The Biograph
Thomas

SILENT LEADER

By Rodney Brown

Brown Publishing LLC
Rochester, New York

1

ISBN-978-0-9864195-0-8

First Edition, copyright 2015

Edited by Brown Publishing LLC

Cover design created by Rodney Brown

Cover design applied by Phu Concepts

Brown Publishing books are available at special quantity discounts to use as premiums and sales promotions or for use in educational programs and educational settings. For more information, please write to Director of Special Sales, Brown Publishing LLC.

Brown Publishing LLC, 518 W. Main Street, Rochester, New York 14608 or call (585) 484-0432.

The author's wish is to thank LaShay Harris-project manager and Phu Concepts-production team.

Preface

The idea for this book began when our local reporter, Mr. Rodney Brown interviewed me about the achievements of my late husband, Dr. Freddie Thomas. I suggested he should interview some of his friends, associates and coworkers.

Surprisingly, over one hundred commented about how Dr. Thomas, (also known as Brother Freddie or just Freddie) influenced their lives in significant ways. You will learn from their hearts, incredible personal and fascinating experiences.

Besides oral research, Rodney conducted archival research surrounding the scientific discoveries made by Freddie and his inventions. This inspired him to write more about the late Freddie Thomas.

I am fascinated about Rodney Brown's writing skills. He easily maneuvers us through captivating journeys from one era to another without the reader recognizing the transition.

He leads us on a journey throughout Freddie's childhood into his experiences of education, inventions, music, lectures, mentoring and a two and a half year illness into his final days. Many of his stories are relevant to happenings not only in Rochester, but also throughout social and political environments in the United States. I am honored, my new adopted son, Mr. Rodney Brown wrote and produced: *Silent Leader.*

I welcome you to express your comments anytime about me and the late Freddie Thomas @ www.drfreddiethomas.com and Facebook.com *@Silent Leader*

Sincerely,

Midge Thomas

Acknowledgements

I value and appreciate those who participated in the success of publishing this book as well as other Freddie Thomas Legacy involvements.

Beverly Randall	Dana K. Miller
Jo Ann Session	Ruthie Baines
William Johnson Jr.	Joe Swift
Helen Corley	Louise Owens
Louise Slaughter	Dave Gantt
Sylvia Barker	John M. Griffin
LuDog Freedman	Jeannette Dunlap
John Walker	Trialfa Omega
Mike Lubas	Earl Washington
Jeron Rogers	Juanita Parello
Joan Howard Coles	William Lewis
Earnest Lofton	Rev. Jerry McCullough
Mia Hodgins	Willie Miles
Dr. Walter Cooper	Ron Thomas

LaShay Harris   Martha Hope

Phu Concepts   Betty Anderson

Earnest Miller   Theresa Prioleau

Tony Brown   Ann Brown

Shirley Harris   Baden Street Settlement

I know for sure, the dedication each of you contributed in various ways to me and the legacy of Dr. Freddie Thomas, humbled and spiritually pleases him very much,

Midge Thomas

Personal testimonies by Dr. Thomas's students, friends and associates include:

- Adams, Archie, (former technical writer), Bausch & Lomb, Rochester, New York
- Barker, Silvia, (storyteller), Rochester, New York
- Beyah, Charles, (former educator), Rochester City School District, Rochester, New York
- Bibby, Peter, (former director), Rochester Police Civilian Review Board, Rochester, New York
- Cato, David John, PhD, (former professor), Colgate Rochester Crozer Divinity School, Rochester, New York
- Cooper, Walter PhD, (community activist and former scientist) at Eastman Kodak and Regent Emeritus of the state of New York
- Coles Howard Joan, (former editor and publisher) of Frederick Douglas Voice, Rochester, New York
- Daniels, Ray, (former owner) of Ray Daniels Barber Shop, Rochester, New York

- Eck, Perry, MD, (Freddie's former physician), Fairport, New York

- Gantt, David, New York (Assembly Member) District 137, Rochester, New York

- Goldstein, David, PhD., (former Scientist) University of Rochester, Department of Radiation Biology and Biophysics, Rochester, New York

- Griffin, John, (former president) of The Freddie Thomas Foundation and The Triangle Community Center, Rochester, New York

- Gifford, Bernard, PhD., a graduate of the University of Rochester, Department of Radiation Biology and Biophysics, (professor of education), University of California Berkeley, Berkeley, California

- Hamlett, Herb, (former radio show host) of The Herb Hamlett Radio Show, Rochester, New York

- Lee, Walter, (filmmaker), Rochester, New York

- Lewis, William, (former principal), Rochester City School District

- McCullough, Jerry, (pastor) of Faith Temple Apostolic

Church, Rochester, New York

- Miles, William, (attorney), Wilmington, North Carolina

- Mitchell, Constance, (community activist), former Monroe County Legislature and Third Ward Supervisor, Rochester, New York

- Moxley, Myron, (entrepreneur), Rochester, New York

- Rogers, Jeron, (civil engineer), Rochester, New York

- Scofield-Hope, Martha, (president) of Rochester Genesee Valley Club of The National Association of Negro Business and Professional Women's Clubs Inc.

- Spady, James, (historian and curator) of the Black History Museum, Philadelphia, Pennsylvania

- Thomas, Midge, (widow) of Dr. Freddie Thomas, Rochester, New York

- Washington, Earl, (entrepreneur), Gibsonville, North Carolina

Foreword

Drawing on his varied experiences and knowledge of the long struggle of African Americans for total emancipation and opportunity in the United States, the author has written an insightful book of the life and career of Freddie Thomas.

The author delineates how the philosophy of origins of the black race, knowledge and ideology helped shape the life of the subject. These principles dominated the life and teachings of the subject and were used to teach individuals, the guiding values in their revival of the racism and oppression that dominated their lives.

Individuals who represented a variety of organized factions accepted the basic tenets of the author's subject. The principles of the subject as highlighted by Rodney Brown are indisputable to the mental, educational and economic liberation of African Americans.

-Walter Cooper, PhD, is a former scientist (Eastman Kodak) and Regent Emeritus of the state of New York.

"Know thyself and you will know how to please the Lord"-
Dr. Freddie Thomas

Freddie was fascinated with his findings after reading a
book that explains the field of natural science, which deals
with the description, prediction, and understanding of the
natural phenomena.

He was excited to learn more about unfamiliar organisms;
he'd discovered while playing outdoors. Freddie
demonstrated an interest in reading and could be found
studying volume after volume on numerous subjects at an
early age. This insatiable quest for information served him
quite well in his later career as a research technologist.

Freddie was born in 1918 and reared to maturity in the
town of Berkeley, a small segregated community in
Norfolk, Virginia. By the start of World War I, every
Southern state had passed Jim Crow laws, using the 1896
case of Plessy v. Ferguson.

The United States Supreme Court upheld the Louisiana
law, ruling that established separate-but-equal public
accommodations and facilities was a reasonable exercise of
the police power of a state to promote the public good.

Under the laws of Jim Crow, African Americans and whites

could not ride together in the same railroad cars, sit in the same waiting rooms, use the same washrooms, eat in the same restaurants or sit in the same theaters.

African Americans were also denied access to parks, beaches, picnic areas and many hospitals.

Freddie's life as a kid growing up in a southern state is synonymous to living behind the Iron Curtain. The political, military and ideological barrier erected by the Soviet Union (today Russia) after World War II was dubbed the Iron Curtain because its aim was to seal off itself and its dependent eastern and central European allies from open contact with the western countries and other noncommunist areas.

Beside the community of black churches it was very few places of refuge for African Americans. The churches were held in high regards because of its role as a place of worship and a place of gathering.

The church represented 'hope' for the citizens of African ancestry living in America. And from this platform, organizations including the Universal Negro Improvement Association (UNIA) and the National Association for the Advancement of Colored People (NAACP) began to take root in Norfolk, Virginia's African American communities.

The distinctive approaches by the organizations to secure equal rights and higher economic standards for people of color were in complete opposition. The job of W.E.B. Dubois, NAACP's director of publicity and research was to promote equality of rights and to eradicate caste or race prejudice among the citizens of the United States, by using the nation's judicial system as a basis to file civil rights litigations.

Marcus Mosiah Garvey, the charismatic leader of the UNIA, blamed America's judicial system for creating laws that fostered inequality and believes African Americans would never be accepted as equals in the United States. Garvey pushed for African Americans to develop their own separate communities or even migrate back to Africa.

In comparison, the NAACP during the 1920s failed to penetrate the consciousness of large masses of African Americans, as did the UNIA. In May of 1917, Garvey established UNIA's headquarters in New York City with 13 members. By 1920, the UNIA had 1,900 chapters in 40 countries around the world. Most of the divisions were located in the United States. By 1926, the membership had grown to over 6 million members.

"God and nature first made us what we are and then out of our own created genius we make ourselves what we want to be. Follow always that great law. Let the sky and God be our limit and eternity our measurement"-Marcus Garvey

The annually held UNIA conventions opened with parades in Harlem, New York that featured more than 100,000 people of color marching down the streets. Members of various UNIA programs wore uniforms and marched proudly as the finest examples of black excellence, discipline and unity.

The parades featured the Black Cross Nurses, Universal African Motor Corps, Universal African Legion, Juveniles Legion and also cultural and artistic groups, bands and international division representatives, all in full ceremonial dress.

Members of the male Universal African Legion studied military discipline as well as the geography of Africa, mathematics, reading and writing and other subjects. The African Black Cross Nurse was modeled after the American Red Cross. Some members had formal medical training, but most worked with practical training in first aid and nutrition.

Because people of color were barred from many hospitals, the members performed benevolent community work and provided public health-service including infant health and home care in minority neighborhoods.

Members of the female Universal African Motor Corps were trained in automobile driving and repair as well as military discipline. The Black Eagle Flying Corps were trained as airplane pilots. And the juvenile divisions were divided into groups according to age.

The infant class ages 1-7 studied the Bible, the doctrine of the UNIA and the history of Africa. After the age of 7, the children were segregated by sex. Girls were taught sewing and the boys' learned about woodcraft. However both received further instruction in Black History, economics, etiquette and various disciplines of science.

After the age of 13, the boys received military training before joining the African Legion, while girls learned hygiene and domestic science before joining the Black Cross Nurse.

Children of the organization were encouraged to pursue advanced degrees within the scientific, medical and engineering fields and become ministers of the African Orthodox Church.

The majority of African American females of working age were at the bottom tiers of domestic jobs, before the UNIA was formed. Many of them were drawn to the organization to explore opportunities denied to them in the larger society.

The UNIA provided a space in America, where women of African ancestry could gain the respect of their peers, by being able to achieve different levels of leadership.

Freddie's grandmother, a Black Cross Nurse, enrolled him in the organization's preparatory school at the age of four. After the passing of Freddie's mother from an unknown illness, his grandmother played a maternal role in his life.

Senior members of the UNIA began to work with Freddie independently, when he began to show he was far more academically inclined than his peers.

Outside of the UNIA, his grandmother worked as a cook for a Jewish family and at times Freddie would tag along to play with their grandson, Aharon. When Freddie found out his middle name was of Jewish origin and was inspired by an event that happened in the Bible, his interest in the Jewish culture peaked.

The African Orthodox Church was established in the belief that Black Episcopalians should have a denomination of their own. While they believe God has no color, yet is human to see everything through one's own spectacles. The faith is steeped in black symbolism that created God, angels, and the prophets in the image of African people.

His grandmother revealed to him an allegory in the Bible that spoke of God's command to Moses to single out first-born males to serve as the nation's priests. The men were to be protected by God's Grace from any harm as they traveled among the people to spread his message of Faith and Obedience.

These men together constituted the Tribe of Levi, which is pronounced like your middle name, but spelled with the letter (I) instead of (Y) at its ending," his grandmother told Freddie.

Freddie started to show more gravitas towards various religions, after being told the Bible inspired his middle name.

When he didn't tag along with his grandmother, Freddie spent portions of the day collecting insects and small mammals of every description, he could find.

After collecting a few, he would head home to his makeshift laboratory (an old chicken coop in the backyard), to dissect them and study their anatomy. Freddie was small for the average tween, but not short on confidence.

He was very sociable and surprisingly well versed for a kid. During those years, a cultural movement in New York City coined as the Harlem Renaissance (1917-1928) began to introduce revolutionary ideas.

The movement challenged America's racial caste system through the production of literature, art and music.

His uncles, Alfred and Leroy made frequent trips to find temporary work in Harlem. When the jobs ended, the two would head back to Norfolk with stacks of books for Freddie to read. The literary works were templates for racial consciousness, where black writers expressed the uniqueness of their race compared to others, in terms of physical characteristics, history, culture and traditions.

The movement energized Harlem and beyond with its race-conscious and class-conscious demands for political equality, and an end to segregation and lynching.

Freddie was intrigued by the readings and the sheer thought, a place like Harlem existed. The assortment of literature written by black artists also ignited his love for poetry.

To raise money, he collected cardboard boxes, measured and scissor out 5'x 5' inch squares, spray painted them black, before writing original acrostic love poems on them.

L. O. V. E.

(AN ACROSTIC)

L ove is an eternal beauty,

O wing its existence to God,

V irtue is its eldest child,

E ternal happiness is its reward.

Freddie Thomas, age twelve

Freddie sold the poems in town to any passerby for five cents. Over a period of years working odd jobs here and there, he had saved enough money to travel to New York City, to buy books he couldn't find in libraries that were located in the southern states.

Freddie would later imply in his writings that, "When he was a kid, public libraries in southern states had no history of black people in the section called History. It has in it the history of the common housefly. However nothing on you and me. You will have to go to the section called sociology to read anything about us, which means we are viewed only as a social problem."

"To know who you are, you must know who you are not. Otherwise you cannot make a proper distinction"-Dr. Freddie Thomas

Freddie visited New York City for the first time in the summer of 1931. A member of the UNIA met him at the bus terminal. They commuted to the organization's headquarters, a large two-story building that was furnished with a Race History Library and stacked with volumes of books explaining the many disciplines of science.

Freddie's visit continued with a tour through the city's historic libraries and museums, before heading to the National Memorial African Bookstore on 7th Avenue. The bookstore's owner Lewis H. Michaux is credited for stimulating a generation of students, intellectuals, writers and artists.

Malcolm X wrote his speeches in the back of his store and it's widely known that Michaux supported Marcus Garvey.

Other regular visits included W.E.B. Dubois, Paul Roberson, A. Philip Randolph and Thurgood Marshall.

In many historical accounts, the store has been deemed as an important reading room of the civil rights movement. It was a rare place for black people and scholars and anyone interested in literature by or about African Americans, Caribbean and South Americans.

Michaux encouraged his visitors to begin their own libraries. However those short of money were allowed to sit down and read.

Some of the books that Freddie bought from the store were rare and irreplaceable. After the Great Depression in America, lasting from 1929 to 1939, many books published during that period were never reprinted.

The tour ended at the Schomburg Center for Research in Black Culture. The Schomburg Center, an archive repository for information on people of African ancestry worldwide is a division of the New York City Public Library that's located in the Harlem section of Manhattan.

In the early part of the 20th century, the library decided to focus on preserving books written by blacks to enhance its African American collection. The library's primary researcher Arturo Schomburg, an important figure in the Harlem Renaissance once edited Negro World, a weekly newspaper established in New York City, as the voice of the UNIA.

Some historians suggest Schomburg was interested in selling his collection of African American literature, only if the person who decided to buy the collection donates it back to the library and make it available to the general public.

After his initial visit to New York, Freddie continued to travel back and forth to buy books and spend time among the Schomburg Collection.

The books and artifacts were scrambled in an assembled area. They never made chronological provisions by which you would have, the outlet of contributions to study. Freddie would comb through troves of historical findings among the collection and other resource centers he was led to as a result of specific studies by Schomburg.

In less than a month, Freddie was familiar with museums and libraries that existed in New York City, as he was with his own home. And after each visit, he shared what he'd uncovered with his boyhood friend Cecil Rhodes.

When the two are together, they become staunch adventurers like Tom Sawyer and Huckleberry Finn. Cecil's dad established a five-bed dental hospital in Norfolk, which is said to be the second one in the United States and the first dentistry established by a person of minority status. The hospital was fully equipped and served all classes alike. After graduating from Booker T.

Washington High School, Freddie decided to study biology at Virginia State College, by way of correspondence courses because of the state's segregation laws.

By not having to be physically in class allowed him the flexibility to continue a weekly library discussion in his hometown. The lectures he delivered at those gatherings are intended to disclose the role of the Negro race in world history, particularly regarding political and social movements.

"The discussions were conducted in current workshop style allowing members of the audience to cut in occasionally with a question or a comment, on the point under consideration," The Norfolk Journal and Guide reported. "Mrs. J.P. Giddings, field representative of the UNIA, directed the discussions and furnished additional data on various questions, which were raised."

Freddie gave an interesting account of the career of Henri Christophe, ruler of Haiti. Much of the discussion centered on the grandeur of the defense fortress built by the sovereign.

The Citadel built after 1811 is listed as one of the Seven Wonders of the World. It stands on top of a mountain on the Haitian coast known as the Bishop's Hat, 2,5000 feet above sea level in the heart of jungle country, about 14 miles south of Cape Haitian.

Freddie noted that Haitians gained their independence through military and diplomatic victory over their enslavers, before Americans secured their independence.

Freddie was a very good orator. He understood the power of knowledge and its purpose to be shared. He could connect words brilliantly and it wouldn't go over your head. He wanted you to be self-taught, able to research, be inquisitive and able to seek knowledge on your own.

When speaking to kids, Freddie would set the format and lay it out for them. He would research the materials two to three times over on each point, to be able to further clarify and simplify what he was talking about.

He would talk about who they are, and how they were wasting their time trying to be something they're not. He was telling them to be themselves. He was trying to transform their minds from self-degradation and self-hatred, to love of self, and acknowledgment of your worth as a human being and the creative talents that could emanate from that fundamental humanity.

In the days of perpetual segregation, Freddie saw a generation of black youth riddled of self-pride and understood the world wasn't going to change and they were the ones that have to change.

It was philosophical, but also mind changing of getting people to look at themselves in a different light, in terms of historical perspective. He would tell his young audiences that they didn't come from people swinging from trees, but from dynamic communities thousands of years old.

His teachings radiated a belief suggesting that no one can degrade you as a human being, if you know who you are as a human being and nobody can destroy your confidence, if you really believe in your humanity.

"A bird cannot fly before it is feathered, pin feathered at that,"-Dr. Freddie Thomas

He was appointed Secretary General of UNIA's Norfolk's faction in 1943. The division recorded an immediate boost in membership, especially among youth during his tenure.

The renewed popularity did not come without increased surveillance from local authorities. For men, if the authorities had your name and address and were a member of the UNIA, you would lose your job.

Freddie was prepared to continue his work with the organization, despite growing threats from the local police force. However his grandmother had other plans. She considered it as an opportune time for Freddie to make good on his promise, to not abandon his goal to become the family's first doctor.

Freddie delivered his final presentation, *Books and the Importance of Research*, on June 23, 1945.

The program celebrated the establishment of a Race History Library at the local UNIA Hall. The Norfolk Journal and Guide reported O.C. Stevenson, chair of the library committee, who presided at the dedicatory program explained the purpose of the library.

Other speakers included the Reverend A. E. Johnson and L.L. Booth, president of the local UNIA.

Mrs. Giddings reminded the audience that, "Any group is racially dead, when it does not know its history and the late Marcus Garvey, before his death requested that reading rooms be opened in various cities, where UNIA locals exist, so that black people can read of their past and thus know what their race has done in the development of world civilizations."

The following week, Freddie enrolled at Wagner College in Staten Island, New York.

The medical school was founded in 1883 in Rochester, New York, as the Rochester Lutheran Pro-seminary. Wagner relocated to Grymes Hill on Staten Island in 1918.

African Americans seeking a medical education were faced with difficult prospects in the late 19th century and much of the 20th century. Few medical schools would admit black students, regardless of their academic excellence. Wagner officials began to reach out to students of color during the mid-1940s.

Freddie and John Lewis, a student from Philadelphia, Pennsylvania were the first person of color to be accepted. Freddie was able to live with his dad, who had remarried and moved to Staten Island. So, unlike most incoming African American freshmen into a predominately white college, student housing was not an issue.

Freddie continued to accept invitations to speak at youth oriented events, including seminars and workshops. His trove of knowledge complimented with an unbridled rhetorical style, opened the door for countless opportunities.

The Staten Island Youth Council of the NAACP organized many of the events, where he spoke. And unlike his lectures in Norfolk, he was introduced as Freddie Thomas, a pre medical student at Wagner College, with no mention of having any association with the UNIA.

To him it felt natural as he crossed a maturation point, where an organization was not the determining factor for opportunities to stimulate an appreciation of the African Diaspora and other people of color's contribution to civilization.

The meetings were usually held on Fridays at 8pm in the Port Richmond Library. During a discussion held on August 10, 1949, the Staten Island Advance reported that Freddie gave an interesting account called *Negro History, from Ancient to Modern Times.*

Within the presentation he declared, the colored race originated in the Pacific area and not in Africa, as it is commonly believed today. He also declared that references to the Negro's presence in America before arrival of Christopher Columbus were found in a diary kept by the explorer.

"Negroes were the first inhabitants of Palestine, Egypt and India," Freddie added. "Many authorities claim Jesus Christ, Krishna, a Hindu God of India were Negroes."

Freddie continued to make a comparison between the lives of Christ and Krishna, the newspaper reported.

"Also in the religious field," he said. "Many historians agree that Akhenaten, a Negro is the father of monotheism instead of Moses."

Included in the list of famous Negro men given by him were Aesop and Lohkman, two great fabulists of ancient times. And Imhotep: A Negro who played an important role in laying the foundation of medicine. Also mentioned were liberators and rulers of Haiti, including Toussaint L'Ouverture, Dessalines, Petion and Christophe.

"In another phase, Freddie told the group some of the history of the defeat of Dhu Nuwas, Yeminite King by Abraha, leader of the Christian Ethiopians, thereby starting a Christian-Mohammmedan war which lasted over a 1,000 years," the newspaper reported.

Freddie implied to the audience that "Just as long as World History does not include that of the Negro, the Negro people must keep it alive."

Freddie always shared authentic documents and books that validated his research after each lecture.

At the start of his senior year, he was nominated to become a Rhodes scholar. Because of the Scholarship's Eponym Cecil Rhodes's interest in Britain's quest to colonize South Africa, Freddie resented the recognition.

He successfully completed the requirements to earn a Bachelor of Science degree in 1950, before enrolling at Albany Medical School in Albany, New York.

Unlike his college days at Wagner, his white colleagues ostracized him. Freddie's haphazard tendency to introduce information about the achievements of people of African ancestry in the field of medicine seem to always spark a debate among his classmates.

In one discussion Freddie shared four pioneering facts surrounding the field of medicine and its connection to the continent of Africa.

• It is reported by Clement of Alexandria that Moses learned medicine from the Egyptians

• Plato and Eudoxus spent 13 years of study with priests of Egypt who were very learned in astronomy and medicine, but very mysterious and uncommunicative. The priests hid from them the greater part of their knowledge

• Athothis, the son and successor of Menes, founder of the First Dynasty was a physician and wrote books on medicine. The first book was a text on anatomy and the dissection of the human body. This is said to be the first anatomy treatise ever written

• The term *chemistry* is derived from *Chemi,* meaning (Black Land), the ancient name for Egypt. The science itself was called, Black Art.

The precise information of African men as pioneers in the field of medicine baffled his colleagues. Freddie was always forced to go to the trunk of his car and return with three standard size briefcases, full of books and materials.

Upon returning, he would tell his doubters, "I didn't bring this for me, I brought if for those of you who want to challenge me. I know you're not used to accepting the authentic backing of a black person and you got to have other people authenticate it for you to accept it."

When he needed to get away from the daily bustle of college life, Freddie spent time visiting friends in Rochester, New York.

Rochester is well known for its ties to former slave, abolitionist, orator, and publisher Frederick Douglass, who made his home there in 1847.

As early as 1810, freed blacks were living in Western New York and soon established Rochester's first African American neighborhood located on High Street that later became Clarissa Street.

The neighborhood was located in the Third Ward. Twenty years later, Reverend Thomas James, an escaped slave, found the Memorial African Methodist Episcopal Zion Church in 1830.

The church became an essential hub for the Underground Railroad, Douglass's abolitionist newspaper (The North Star) and for Susan B. Anthony's women's suffrage movement.

A slow progressive flow of stable black families continued to move into the Third Ward with each passing decade. During the Great Depression general unemployment was 40 percent and among blacks 70 percent, but they were able to keep their families together.

The Third Ward had a sound population composed of upward mobile families like the Dubois, Stevens, Grays, Coles, and Walls. You had two doctors, Lunsford and Jordan, two dentists-Lindsey and Levy, and two morticians-Latimore and Myers. The Third Ward's stable population would abruptly change following a massive migration of black people fleeing the South.

Rochester is home to several pioneering companies, including Eastman Kodak, Bausch & Lomb, Xerox and Rochester Products Division, an auxiliary of General Motors.

Those fleeing the South considered Rochester, an ideal destination because of its history of progressive social justice and reputation for migrant jobs. The city of Rochester in 1945 had a population of 5,000 black people. By 1964, almost 32,000 black people lived in Rochester, with the greater percentage arriving from the South.

A number of settlement houses were organized in Rochester, such as Baden Street in 1901, to ease the transition of people migrating from all parts of Europe. Several years later, the Genesee Settlement House and Lewis Street Center were established to accommodate the continuous influx of Jewish, Italian, and Russian immigrants.

The goals set by the houses were to *"pursue the elimination of the causes of poverty and to reduce the level of negative social problems associated with being disadvantaged."*

During the massive migration of black people from 1945 to 1960, no community instrument existed in Rochester to ease the transition. The only accessible instrument was Baden Street beginning to move into the area of serving African Americans.

The newcomers largely settled in the Third and Seventh Wards. The Seventh Ward with Joseph Avenue at its heart was the only neighborhood with public housing in the 1950s. Most African Americans lived in a 12-block area in the Third Ward and a 12-block area in the Seventh Ward, where many dilapidated housings were concentrated.

Third Ward resident Constance Mitchell said, "Rochester had a very low unemployment rate but jobs were not available. The factories were not open to minorities.

"It was well known, if minorities applied for jobs in the factories their applications would end up in File 13-the wastebasket," she said.

"People coming to Rochester from the southern states weren't aware of the struggles, so they kept coming. And when Freddie started coming around, the black population in Rochester was beginning to realize, if they were to control anything to a certain degree it would be within their own communities."

Other than turning their focus towards community development to establish social mobility, African Americans in Rochester had few options to improve their livelihoods.

By the mid-1950s, Clarissa Street had become a main commercial district of the Third Ward. Businesses included the Gibson Hotel, Latimer Funeral Home, Ray Daniel Barbershop, Scotty Pool Hall, Smitty Birdland, LaRue and Pendleton Restaurants and the Vallot Tavern, just to name a few.

The Third Ward nightclubs such as the Pythodd Club, the Elk Club and Dan Restaurant and Grill, became famous for jazz music. Grocery stores, bakeries, pharmacies, and clothing shops, occupied both sides of Jefferson Avenue. And across-town, Joseph Avenue became a main commercial district where minorities were majority stakeholders.

The black community was transformed into one big family. They were conscious of behaving kindly to each other.

They were being black, buying black and thinking black. A unity compelled by segregation.

The atmosphere in Rochester coincided with books written during the Harlem Renaissance that Freddie read as a kid. The presence of racial pride and bustling minority-owned businesses was reminiscent of the period. Freddie described his arrival in the city in 1952 as, "Finding Heaven."

"I came to Rochester to visit a fraternity brother of mine," Freddie recalls. "It was so peaceful here, I stayed for three days.... then a week.... then two weeks.... then I jumped in my car to get my belongings from New York City and move myself here."

He found refuge at the Young Men Christian Association (YMCA) on Gibbs Street. The building's 216 rooms fulfilled the YMCA's mission to provide young men new to the city with a wholesome home away from home. Freddie didn't return to Albany Medical School after arriving in Rochester in 1952.

Freddie preferred studying alone. He had been forced to all his life because of his skin color. Wherever there was a school or program he could correspond with, Freddie would enroll in programs that included anthropology, paleontology, archeology and other subjects of interest.

Much of his knowledge was derived from information obtained from research. Along with acclaimed author J. A. Rogers, Freddie pioneered in the research of black global distribution, especially in Asia.

Before becoming a national figure, Rogers wrote periodically for Negro World, a UNIA publication. Roger's book, *From Superman to Man* was self-published in 1917 that attacked notions of African inferiority made an indelible impression on Freddie as a teenager.

The book's arguments against what fuels racism is pulled from many sources, classical and contemporary, and run the gamut from history and anthropology to biology.

Rogers and Freddie would often exchange information and on a number of occasions, Freddie would carry bundles of newspapers and magazine clippings for use in Roger's multi-volume, *Sex and Race.*

Freddie didn't want any credit for his contributions. He was a person of great knowledge, who had a vision how to pass it on to others. Freddie would later imply in his writings that, the root word of university is universe, so knowledge is not to be taught behind closed walls, but also to anyone and everyone in the universe who seeks. Freddie believed it's not knowledge, unless you share it with someone.

In a letter to Rogers dated December 10, 1952, Freddie writes:

"I am continuing my research on the African in medicine, as you know, I run across material, you may use in your work, as well. I do not wish to burden you with data already in your possession. Therefore, I am listing some facts, I have uncovered. From these, you may select those that you don't have at this time, when you so desire. I will forward, the references. These and other facts are in my possession and you may draw freely from my collection, whenever you so desire."

The Philosophy

By the mid 1950s, Freddie had amassed hundreds of rare books and documents of historical importance. He was always giving people stuff to read. He had a library in the trunk of his car. And soon began to set up public exhibits on the street corners of downtown to share rare commodities from his private collection.

Freddie's base of knowledge was broad. And to call him a giant is no overstatement. He was heavy in science, mathematics, religion, history and a host of other fields. His knowledge ran deep.

Freddie was a scholar and was driven to share what he knew with whoever showed any interest in wanting to learn. If I had to pick an area where his greatest interest lay, I would have to conclude, he was more interested in those areas having specific significance to people of color. To say this does not detract from the other areas of his interest, for he had a way of connecting people of African ancestry into all spheres of knowledge.

He lived, studied and taught life from the perspective of a black person.

The growing number of people clamoring to hear him

speak was a measurement to his popularity. The YMCA prepared a spacious room, where he could give lectures to accommodate his growing number of visitors. Freddie's search for other outlets to educate the public led him to Saint Simon Episcopal Church at 6 and a ½, Oregon Street.

There he met, Dr. Walter Cooper, a research scientist at Eastman Kodak; teaching Black History to high school students using E. Franklin Frazier's book, *History of the Negro in the United States.*

In reflection of that evening, Dr. Cooper remembered that everything was all right with the kids, until he started talking about slavery.

"The students became shameful," Cooper, recall. "They didn't understand we weren't people who accepted slavery. And the fact that there were more than 200-slave revolts. I think psychologically, the system imposed upon us guilt for their brutality and we've accepted it. It's why we don't look at our history of being enslaved clearly," Cooper continued.

"When I met Freddie, he was very interested in bioscience and we became close friends. Freddie confined his ideology to individuals. He was an expert in spreading knowledge depicting early civilizations inhabited by people of color, combined with religious information and experience. He was dabbing into more of the early history of the Middle Eastern part of the World and I was more of what black people experienced in the United States," Cooper pointed out.

"I started at the beginning of slavery in America, however the historical process goes back much earlier than that. It was kind of a different approach, but there were no conflicts between us. I believe that, the new generation of black students had to understand America to the point, where they could arrive at a position to branch out and try to understand the world. Freddie's philosophy implied that, academic success and social mobility could be generated by showing how early knowledge in this universe was often generated by people of color. And he would talk about the destruction of the library in Alexander, Egypt," Cooper noted.

"He talked about the Moors and the contribution they made to agriculture, technology, architecture and writings that I thought were good. So Freddie and I would often talk about things. I considered him as more of a Garveyite (a follower of Marcus Garvey) with the early history and origins of knowledge more so than the African American Experience here in the United States, which I projected. I always felt it was necessary to be able to escape the fundamental racism, here in the United States. I believed if you could escape, you could always go back and broaden your knowledge of the historical perspective."

"But Freddie believed, the origins might be more important than at some later period in history. And looking at the result as they had an impact on African Americans, I think Freddie could've been right. I think attempts through writings, whether it was Dubois's, Baldwin's or James Weldon's music, they all had an impact in a way that somehow wasn't significant enough to get African Americans to change their modality of thinking about themselves. Nor did the seminal work of Kenneth Clark and Maime Clarke, who did the original black doll, brown doll, white doll study in 1948, which spurred into a publication in 1950: *Emotional Factors in Racial Identification and Preference in Negro Children*."

"Blacks go through a period of civil rights rebellion and sloganeering phases like "black is beautiful.' However, 40 years later, you run the same study and nothing have changed. So it's something the mind thinks to be impenetrable reality, you're a human being," Cooper said.

Former Princeton University Professor Kwame Anthony Appiah did an interesting research on the history of his native country Ghana and its Ashanti population. The Ashanti were the dominant tribe who kept other Africans enslave until 1807, when the British outlawed slavery in the colonies.

Professor Appiah wondered what happened to the descendants of the former slaves? What is their attitude today toward the Ashanti Tribe? He found out there were no researchable difference of the descendants than their former ancestral slave foreparents. They still felt they were inferior and showed deference to members of the Ashanti Tribe in every facet of life.

Appiah wondered how 400 hundred years (20 generations) later there's no attitude change. The only conclusion he could draw is that it's a conditional response transmitted from generation to generation as if it is transcript in their DNA.

"Now the assignment for all of us is to go back to the social-psychology of the slave plantation," Cooper said. "What was it? What did it create? Then, review contemporary African Americans today. Do you see the same behavioral patterns?

We are the ones who have to change and Freddie honored it. Freddie understood that in order to penetrate centuries of psychological enslavement it was necessary to teach from a historical perspective to have any success in transforming the mind of blacks from self-degradation and self-hatred, to love of self and acknowledgment of your worth as a human being.

Freddie's philosophy suggests you are free, if your mind is determined, you are free."

"There's no work more sacred than the liberation of the black people. I must constantly avail myself to this cause or report to my God, the reason why"-Dr. Freddie Thomas

Beating the many odds stacked against persons of color, Freddie was hired by Eastman Kodak as a research technologist in 1952.

He was assigned to work in the Emulsion and Research Division, which is the most sensitive and critical division of Kodak's research labs.

Freddie was the only black scientist assigned to work in the highly regarded department.

The American National Standards Institute says, "The most fundamental layer in a film is the emulsion layers. The emulsion is the photographic part of the film that consists of dispersions of light-sensitive materials in a colloidal medium, usually gelatin, carried as a thin layer on a film base. It's made by dissolving silver bullion in nitric acid to form silver-nitrate crystals. These crystals are dissolved and mixed with other chemicals to form silver-halide grains and then suspended in the gelatin emulsion coating. The size and degree of light sensitivity of these grains determines the speed or amount of light required to register an image."

What came out of Kodak's Emulsion and Research Division comprised all the chemistry and physics that dominated the film process. The position required a person highly skilled in the methodology of chemistry and photographic science.

With a decent paying job under his belt, Freddie moved to 439 and 1/2 Tremont Street in 1953. The small, one bedroom apartment was in proximity to bustling black-owned businesses and taverns that dominated the corridors of Jefferson Avenue and Clarissa Street.

Freddie's visits to Ray Daniels barber shop sped up his acculturation into Rochester's black communities. It was a regular hangout for him to discuss and answer questions about Africa and Afro-American History.

"In those days a barbershop was a meeting place where ideas were analyzed, dissected and debated," Daniels said. "Freddie came in for a haircut and we became fast friends. He was a complex, brilliant man, ahead of his time. Our conversations became deeper and to this day his words and my memories of him inspires me."

However Freddie was also concern with a considerable number of high school dropouts susceptible to joining gangs and becoming hustlers that lurked in the shadows of the black community. Freddie saw an urgent need to educate them Daniels noted.

To engage in conversation with teenagers and young adults, Freddie would often visit popular restaurants and pool halls, they routinely attended or simply waited until the bars and clubs closed.

He was willing to stay out and converse all night. It was incomprehensible; a man with that kind of brilliance would be out in the streets at 3 o'clock in the morning educating young revelers.

The brothers may have been drinking, doing drugs and they probably could do some harm to someone in their inebriated or high state of mind. However they're standing there listening to Freddie.

He believed in excellence. He dressed in excellence. He spoke in excellence. Freddie presented himself as a very generous person; he never raised his voice, drink alcohol or smoke. He was soft spoken but firm. No nonsense, no slogans, everything cut-dry and serious. And that's the way he was. He didn't have a commanding presence as far as visibly.

Freddie's commanding presence was his broad base of knowledge and his intellect.

He was in the street shepherding brothers, putting them in corners and educating them on African and Afro American History, science, math and the importance of obtaining a quality education.

It didn't matter who they were. They gave him total respect. The brothers who were hustlers, pimps and hardcore gang members respected him. Kids could be on the corner shooting dice and Freddie would walk in the middle of the group and command respect. And he got it. He was able to judge body language and gauge what approach and what learning would mostly fascinate and engage the person.

If his initial approach towards a potential mentee fell short of triggering a curious response, he would go in another direction. The discussions would last for hours leaving the kids fascinated, inspired and hungry to hear more. Freddie had a scientific mind, so he would break things down step-by-step. Nobody could've challenge him and you didn't want to because you were too busy listening.

"When I was a teenager, he spent a considerable amount of time with my friends and I, encouraging us to become something in life," said Bishop Jerry McCullough, Pastor of Faith Temple Apostolic Church. "I didn't think he knew my name until one day I was rushed to the hospital to treat an injury I suffered in an altercation. I remember him coming into the hospital room with a smile on his face. He gave me an envelope with money in it and some books about the history of Africa and African Americans. I learned a lot about my heritage from those books, which made me proud to be black. And although, he was a scholar in many fields, Freddie didn't have that air about him that normally accompanies education. When he was in our presence, he was one of the boys," McCullough said.

Many folks had given up on youths in the community deemed as delinquents. And they didn't understand how Freddie was able to persuade kids they viewed as perturbed to consider positive endeavors.

"Freddie became our beacon of light," McCullough said.

They were some who walked away from him and said I don't have time for this. However, Freddie never became unraveled and always replied, *"It's all right, I'll talk to you later."*

And he would move on and talk to someone else. He was a man with incredible compassion for people. He thrived on helping you; help yourself. He believed deeply in his philosophy of life. And if there's anyone that lived the way they felt, Freddie did.

His undying commitment to the community to educate and socially develop young black people soon began to gain the support of local black-owned businesses. Lopez Steak House on Jefferson Avenue and other minority-owned businesses across-town on Joseph Avenue allowed their establishments to serve as designated places for youths to interact with him.

"Freddie had an unusual quality and technique of transferring his scholarly discoveries and research so person could easily understand," said Lawrence Lopez, owner of Lopez Steakhouse. "He would come into the restaurant and strike up a conversation. And talk about history and why black people should be proud. Some adults looked at him strangely without ever knowing the impact he was having on young people. And none of them had access to those types of kids."

Through his passion to educate youths, Freddie was able to maintain professional relationships with others of different ethnicities and simultaneously promote and educate the public about the history of black people on a massive scale.

"The History of Africans in Asia has received only scant attention by black writers," said Historian James G. Spady, curator of the Black History Museum in Philadelphia, Pennsylvania. "The first full-length volume on the subject is Joseph E. Harris, *Africa Presence in Asia*. And that deals almost exclusively with some escaped group of African slaves, who settled there. LeGrand H. Clegg has given some attention to the presence of Africans in China and Japan in his exhaustive scholarly article on *Blacks in Ancient America*," Spady noted. "The most extensive published works on the history of blacks in Asia is the series of articles by Freddie published in a Buffalo, New York newspaper called Empire Star, from June 6, 1957 to December 19, 1958."

In one series, Freddie submitted an excerpt declaring, when James Cook, the famous British Navigator explored the Pacific Ocean expanses, he met the descendants of the ancient Africans and Negroid-Mongoloid intermixes.

[In the Polynesians, the famed sailor met the old Queen, Oberea and the King, Tootahah. Cook took some of the lesser chiefs' captive but the islanders' retaliated by taking one of Cook's men captive. The Englishmen were amazed to find the people of the island had a simple, but efficient economic system in operation.

They even had a rate of exchange that functioned in all

trade relations and transactions. Trade was restricted to persons authorized by the law. Captain Cook is credited with his use of fresh fruits and plants to prevent that ancient scourge of the sea, scurvy.

It is quite possible, the astute sailor learned of this technique from the islanders as he probe his way through the then unknown Pacific. The islanders supplied him with such things as onions, cocoanuts and edible grasses. The Tahitians of the Society Islands taught Cook, how to ferment the breadfruit plant and how they played a musical instrument by blowing through their nostrils.

Cook called them nostril flutes, it is said. The foreigner was so impressed; he took down the structure of their musical scale and the fingering technique of the nose flute. The people of Tahiti bathed three times a day. The women cut their hair short. Cook's journal also records a verbal account of Tahitian wrestling and sportsmanship.

It's of importance to note, two of cook's sailors married women of the islands to remain after their ship sailed. They had fled to the mountains with their spouses. However they were captured and returned to the ship.

The ruler of Tahiti at this time was Tubourai Tamaide. When Cook sailed from Tahiti, he took as his guide a

Tahitian named Tupia. Tupia not only acted as guide to show the Englishman the other islands of the Pacific, but also as the go-between in Cook's intercourse with the people of these islands.

It must be recalled; this was nothing new to the culture of Tahiti since they had for centuries roamed the Pacific Ocean in seaworthy canoes. Some of the canoes were up to seventy-feet in length. Often they were at sea as long as three or four weeks at a time.]

Invitations to speak at seminars and workshops were always pouring in. Freddie rarely made time for leisure activities. His sudden decision to attend a neighbor's birthday party is an indicative sign of his spontaneous character. He loved to do things; he wanted to do, when he wanted to do them.

At the party there was approximately 25 to 30 people dancing and enjoying refreshments in the living room. Freddie was interested in his neighbor's friend Margaret Banks. Friends and relatives affectionately called her Midge. On the first slow song of the night called '*Treasure of Love*' by Clyde McPhatter, Freddie asked Midge to dance.

"When we were dancing it just fit," Midge said. "His height

is 5'7" and my height of 5' 2" were perfectly matched. He wanted to know my name and general things about me. And after the party, he invited me to a dance on East Avenue. We finally ended our night at a 24-hour restaurant, where we conversed until 7am."

It only took one date, before the two were inseparable.

"He was a charming person. And he loved people," Midge said. "Even the intellectual part of him was very personable."

They dated for five months. And on Midge's birthday in September of 1956, Freddie proposed. On his birthday, five months later, she received the matching ring.

Midge's father's words of wisdom to Freddie were simple: If he ever got tired of Midge and they were unable to get along, bring her back home. Freddie replied, "No Mr. Banks. You and Mrs. Banks go ahead and make another Midge, I'll take all of them."

They got married on February 9, 1957 at the African Methodist Episcopal Church on Favor Street, where both were members. The wedding took place, one day before Freddie's birthday.

Out of 900 invitations approximately 700 people attended. Freddie, a self-taught pianist began composing music and writing songs at the age of nine.

At the age of 39, he had copyrighted more than seventy musical pieces. So it was no surprise he chose to write and produce '*Give Me Your Hand*' the theme song for their wedding. Bob Warfield sang the piece during the Midge's stroll to the altar.

They decided to cancel plans to spend their honeymoon-visiting relatives and instead fly to Bermuda.

During mornings while Midge slept, Freddie would dedicate two to three hours doing research at the island's library. He was always busy scanning newspapers and clipping articles of all sorts to file away for future reference. This practice was meant to increase the scope of his knowledge and to support his positions. Wherever he went, he bought books, magazines, newspapers, and anything else that appeared of interest to him. His research on the Bermudian population and its ancestors resulted into a journal in 1958 called: *Negro Members of Parliament in Bermuda.*

Freddie knew the value of certain kinds of information. They stayed on the island for three weeks before returning to Rochester. And shortly thereafter, they purchased their first home in the Marketview Heights area at 26 Skuse Street.

The house's living room became a virtual classroom for hundreds of students he tutored. A large piece of cardboard, he painted black; hoisted from the floor by the living room's radiator, was his makeshift chalkboard.

The recreational room was transformed into a library of more than 5,000 books. The room had racks of books from ceiling to floor. Books pertaining to the history and cultures of Africans, Jews, Europeans and Asians adorned every possible space in the room.

You could use anything in his library. But you had to read the books there. The books were rare commodities and were no longer in circulation or being printed. One such book, '*Maxims of Ptah-Hotep*' is believed to be the first book in history by many scholars.

On the book's cover, Freddie writes:

"The oldest known book in the world was written by a Negro. It is the Maxims of Ptah. Ptah was the oldest of the Egyptian Gods and was of African Pygmy origin. The work consists of forty-four poems and was written approximately 3366 B.C."

The Thomases' lived a humble life in their cozy home right up near the train tracks. Freddie earned enough income to buy a home on the outskirts of the city. But he didn't want to be in the suburbs where many black people in Rochester saw as a goal to one-day move.

"He wanted to be near people of color and because we decided to live in the city, we had more money to travel and spend on vacations," Midge said. "If we were in the suburbs, the taxes and the mortgage probably would've prevented or mitigated much of that."

"I started to see more of his mentoring side on Skuse Street," she noted. "It didn't bother me. And it never took away our time. His ambition to educate young people was normal activity to me."

Midge also enjoyed a flourishing career as a successful businesswoman in beauty culture and hat design. But eventually, she turned her interest to leadership training to boost opportunities for young talented women.

Midge and Thelma Phillips establish the Rochester chapter of the National Association of Negro Business and Professional Women's Club on February 2, 1958.

Two of the club's four major goals are to unite and protect the interests of black businesses and professional women in-and-around Rochester. And encourage young black women to go into business and professions.

"Our other two goals are to provide leadership training for black women in the community and act as big sisters to girls 7 to 12 years of age," Midge said.

With her family's background in public service and as the spouse of Freddie Thomas, she was governed by fate to one-day take-on civic responsibilities.

Freddie and Midge one month after engagement to be married
(October 1956)

"If there's a place with activity educational learning has to be going on"-Dr. Freddie Thomas

The scenery of youngsters with tablets and pencils could be seen entering and leaving the Thomases' home at any given time-either day or night. The young men he tutored and mentored were known as, *Freddie Boys*.

Not only was the presence of people a usual occurrence in their home. But also the serving of tea and cookies (and sometimes ice cream and cake) was normal behavior.

"I always set the dinner table with a few more placemats each night because someone would inevitably stop by," Midge said. "Our place was always open to people of all kinds. All hours at night."

During the late 1950s and well into the 1970s, a consciousness to obtain black power was sweeping through urban cities with large minority populations.

Young people of color saw the civil rights movement of their parents and grandparents as out-of-date.

A number of student activists from organizations, including The Student Nonviolent Coordinating Committee (SNCC), The Nation of Islam (NOI) and The Black Panther Party (BPP), precipitated the movement.

These organizations composed of young black people were eager to join something they felt were of their own.

Freddie was acquainted with NOI spokesperson Malcolm X and the group's leader Elijah Muhammad. Freddie's grandmother and Malcolm's father were both community organizers as members of the UNIA.

Malcolm X frequently traveled to Rochester to speak at area colleges and universities, between the years of 1962 and 1965. Freddie was always the first person he would call and visit when in town. Malcolm was fascinated with the rare books and documents Freddie had complied in his library at home.

In 1963, while studying in Freddie's library, Malcolm was tempted to cancel a speaking engagement, due to his unwillingness to part ways with the sanctuary of knowledge.

Although Freddie at times sported the last name X, he chose to operate as an independent lecturer and teacher. Many of his students considered Freddie to be a scholar of both western and eastern theologies. It was important to Freddie to be able to share contested information from a balance perspective using various sources of information provided by different races and cultures.

Freddie didn't proselytize, especially if it's going to get in the way of him being able to mentor a student. His main goal was to educate.

Peter Bibby, former director of Rochester Police Civilian Review Board said, he never went to the Thomases' home until a friend of his was going over there to have Bible study.

"When we got there. There were nine other boys with Bibles and Qurans. But Freddie was not teaching religion and faith. He was teaching intelligence. He was teaching, how you make information work for you." Bibby said.

My thinking was based on the principles of black radicalism. I was saying things like let's tear this town down. But he opened my mind when he asked: *"What was I going to replace it with?"* I thought about it and stop talking.

He was a different kind of role model. Every time I spoke to Freddie, I learned something. He was teaching me how to learn. He helped me understand that there's a relationship to new information and everything I already know. He taught knowledge doesn't travel on a linear path. But travels instead on a circular path because it has a relationship with everything else. Freddie was about helping people learn-to-learn.

"Those types of discussions were fundamental lessons in my journey towards becoming the chairperson of a panel that reviews and make recommendations on alleged misconduct by employees of the Rochester Police Department," Bibby said.

Freddie changed the warring philosophies of many street gangs in Rochester that included members from the Matadors, Casanovas, Noble Men, Undertakers, and Soul Brothers. He was able to expand their understanding of brotherhood to that of a more community-focused approach.

Freddie never said get out the gang or you're going to end up dead or in jail. He talked about the good they can do in the community. The contributions they could make. And the leaders they could become.

"Freddie was a strong male figure in our lives for social, cultural, and academic training," said Charles Beyah, former educator with the Rochester City School District (RCSD) and gang member. "He taught us our history. And how to love ourselves without hating anyone else."

"Freddie knew politics more than anyone around Rochester. And I am sure he advised Minister Franklin Florence with what he was doing," said David Gantt, New York State Assembly Member of 137 District. "Politicians on the national and local level were regular visitors at his home seeking support for their candidacy."

The Civil Rights Act of 1957 was the first civil rights legislation passed since the Reconstruction Era of the late 1800s. The goal of the legislative act was to ensure that all Americans could exercise their right to vote.

Freddie and other black leaders wanted their local representatives to promptly enforce the ruling. Freddie wanted transformational change of America's social and economic policies that unfairly discriminates against people of color. And to do it, he needed political relationships within the chambers of Capitol Hill in Washington, D.C.

Rochester was a city run by Republicans for the greater part of the 20th century. Freddie had known Representative Kenneth B. Keating of New York's 38 District for a number of years in private life. Keating was considered a moderate politician like many New York Republicans of his era.

The Congressman sent a symbolic message to the black community through his effort to force the congressional dining room to embrace integration by inviting Adam Clayton Powell, a black member of the House of Representatives and his wife to join him there for lunch.

Keating announced his intentions to run for the vacant Senate seat of the retiring Irving Ives in 1958.

Freddie invited Keating to an informal tea reception at his home with representatives of the collective black leadership. He believed Keating could be a good advocate to assure the voice of Rochester's black community receives equal attention in Washington.

Keating attended the function as the Thomases' guest of honor with his daughter Judith.

Because of an inaccurate statement of the purpose of the affair was published prior to the event in the Empire State Newspaper, Freddie thought it was important to point out to the attendees that, if black leadership in Rochester would cooperate and work more closely, greater benefits for the black community would accrue.

He then stated that the morning paper said this event was one of some forty Republican leaders of the black community. And wanted the news reporters in attendance to correctly report a statement that read, [because of the varied religious, social and political persuasions and disciplines of all here present, the informal tea and reception of the black community with its distinguished guest, the Honorable Kenneth B. Keating is characterized by its total independence of such religious, social and political persuasions and disciplines].

Leaders of the black community in Rochester were demanding an end to racial segregation.

Determine to see racial discrimination conditions improve in housing, community activist Constance Mitchell announced her intentions to run for Supervisor of the Third Ward in 1961 and won.

"Rochester was a pitfall town when you really stop and think about it," Mitchell said. "Black folks were being exploited by slumlords. Most of the houses were old houses in the Third Ward. They were houses built for big families. But instead, black folks were piled up on top of each other. Slumlords had taken those big old houses, cut them up and made what you call 'efficiency apartments' that was equipped with a refrigerator, a two-burner little stove and a room. Each house had 18 to 20 mailboxes on it. It wasn't much you could do because social services wanted you over there," Mitchell said. "I wanted to see things change and Freddie was a person I could depend on for sound advice and support."

New York Senator Kenneth B. Keating and Dr. Thomas with representatives of Rochester's collective black leadership, answer questions from news reporters at the home of the Thomases.' (October 1958)

Rochester's first congresswoman Judy Weis, New York 38 District, with Ethel Banks (Midge's mother) and women of the Rochester black community meet over tea in the home of the Thomases.' (March 1959)

Midge, Representative Kenneth B. Keating and Dr. Thomas (October 1958)

KEATING for U. S. SENATOR

October 16, 1958

Mr. Freddie L. Thomas
26 Skuse Street
Rochester, New York

Dear Freddie:

Just a note to tell you how much I enjoyed being with you
during my visit to Rochester. It was a fine occasion and
I appreciated the opportunity to renew so many old acquaint-
ances as well as meet a number of new people.

I want you to know how grateful I am for all the good work
you are doing in behalf of my candidacy.

Please give my best to your wife and thank her for the fine
hospitality accorded me.

With warm regards, I am,

Very sincerely yours,

Kenneth B. Keating

mnp

72

JESSICA McC. WEIS
38th District
New York

COMMITTEES:
Government Operations
District of Columbia

Congress of the United States
House of Representatives
Washington, D. C.

February 17, 1961

Mr. Freddie L. Thomas
26 Skuse Street
Rochester, New York

Dear Freddie:

Enclosed is a copy of my statement regarding the recent Rules Committee controversy which I mentioned to you during our telephone conversation.

As I have tried to point out to everyone who raised the civil rights question in connection with this vote, virtually no one in Washington, whether he or she supported or opposed the Rules Committee change, considered the civil rights issue to be involved. This should be fairly obvious from the fact that one of the two new Democrats appointed to the Rules Committee is Congressman Carl Elliott of Alabama, an avowed segregationist, who has voted 100 percent against civil rights legislation.

I am afraid that the civil rights issue was deliberately interjected into this controversy by certain cynical people who knew that it would have great emotional appeal. I consider their action irresponsible, and I could not allow my own judgement to be influenced by it.

Kindest regards.

Very sincerely yours,

Jessica McCullough Weis

dps
Encl.

73

"Water will seek its own level. Become like water"-Dr. Freddie Thomas

Big industries in Rochester like Kodak and Xerox hired very few people of color. The majority of those hired were subjugated and assigned to low-level jobs. Freddie also experienced discriminatory treatment at Kodak, despite his significant position.

In 1960, Freddie designed a makeshift model to improve the mechanisms used for the company's current emulsion operational procedures. The functional demand of the new model he designed is engineered to advance the coupling reaction for various color layers in the film process.

A senior supervisor determined that Freddie's new model would be less efficient than what they currently use. In addition, the supervisor concluded that the new model was too expensive to build at $30,000 dollars. However Kodak covertly built the new machine and hired a German scientist to assemble it.

"The decision was made to hire someone else to assemble the new model without Freddie knowing," Midge said. "They intentionally hid their intentions. Therefore Kodak was credited for the invention and not Freddie. And that was the final straw that convinced Freddie that he should seek employment at an educational institution involved in scientific and medical discoveries, opposed to manufacturing."

After a brief vacation in Hawaii and several months of intense studying, Freddie applied for a position as a research associate at the University of Rochester (U of R).

In 1961, Freddie was hired to a position at the university in the toxicology unit that's located within the department of U of R's School of Medicine and Dentistry. The well-guarded department required clearance from military officials before anyone could enter.

In a report administered by the U of R, "The division was created during World War II, to accommodate the Atomic Energy Project. The project was organized at the request of the United States Army Corps of Engineers. Its purpose was to research and to provide monitoring services and consultation on the health hazards expected to arise at installations, which were working on the development of the atomic bomb," the report noted.

"In addition, certain plans were surveyed periodically to determine radiation and other hazards and recommendations were involved for their safe operations. Film badges and analytical services were provided for plant personnel. A particular responsibility of the Rochester project was the collection and analysis of periodic medical examinations of personnel in plants all over the country involved in atomic production. Research programs were established in two broad fields: the biological effects of external radiation and the toxicity of radioactive and chemical materials."

The personnel performed toxicology for plutonium and uranium in a special building across the street from the medical center. If you go up Elmwood Avenue, the old medical center complex is on your left and there's a little building near the road on the right that leads to the Atomic Energy Commission Annex; where the toxicology work was performed. It's connected to a tunnel that goes under Elmwood Avenue to the medical center.

Freddie worked in the unit for four years, before the name was changed to the Department of Radiation Biology and Biophysics in 1965 to reflect more accurately the scope of its interest.

At Eastman Kodak, Freddie specialized in photographic science. As a research associate at the U of R, his focus was concentrated in the area of cytology (the branch of biology treating of cells with references to structure, functions, multiplication and life history).

Freddie's working hours varied with his research, unlike when he worked at Kodak where the majority of employees work stationary hours on various shifts.

At the U of R, Freddie could leave and return at his own convenience. He wasn't restricted to a rigid work shift. The flexibility of his working hours allowed him to teach a peer counseling class for students studying for their doctorates at the university.

It was never an unusual occurrence to see in his laboratory while he was working at least one young person to whom he was imparting motivation and guidance.

Archie Adams, former technical writer for Bausch & Lomb, said Freddie approached his endeavors in a very unorthodox manner.

To illustrate his unorthodoxy, he recalled an incident that occurred one evening he took Adam to his laboratory. So he could make adjustments in a cytological experiment.

Adams noticed an inflated balloon attached to a piece of tubing, which was connected to the experiment. So he asked Freddie the purpose of the balloon. Freddie responded that he needed a source of a small amount of carbon dioxide for the experiment. So he attached a tube to a balloon, blew the balloon up, clamped the tube and connected it into the experiment. This arrangement eliminated the need to use a large tank of carbon dioxide, which most others would probably have done under the circumstances.

"That experiment demonstrates the type of thinking that was typical of him in so many other areas. He was always finding simple, uncomplicated ways of doing things," Adams said. "Freddie suggested that humans had to be in tune with nature. And that it was unnatural for him to employ complicated schemes to achieve an end that could be best reached in a more simple natural fashion."

"If each one teaches one, soon we will all be educated"-Dr. Freddie Thomas

United States President Dwight D. Eisenhower wanted to stop in for tea at the Thomases' home. During that time the President traveled by train and the track behind the Thomases' home allowed easy access. But Freddie wouldn't allow it.

Black leaders that even included baseball legend Jackie Robinson had also went public with criticisms of Eisenhower and other Republicans insistence on patience in their pursuit of equal civil rights.

Vigorous voter registration drives led by young people of color in urban communities had forced a shift in the political field. Incumbents of the Republican Party were suddenly losing seats to Democrats.

Republican Vice President Richard Nixon lost his run for the United States Presidency to democratic challenger John F. Kennedy in 1960.

Republican Senator Kenneth Keating of New York lost his seat to democratic challenger Robert F. Kennedy in 1964. And in Rochester, the mayoral victory of democratic Challenger Henry E. Gillette set the precedent for change in the region in 1962.

It was the first time a Democrat was elected Mayor of Rochester in more than several decades.

Gillette interacted with Freddie, Constance Mitchell and others who were part of the black sophistication with politics in Rochester. The election of Gillette was a turning point, but not a catalyst for immediate change.

In response to persistent demands from black residents to enforce the recently passed Civil Rights Act of 1964 was answered with a military-styled police crackdown in the Third and Seventh Wards.

"Rochester was being run like a plantation, a controlled city," Peter Bibby said. "Anywhere black people congregated there were officers with K-9 dogs who were given complete discretion to breakup, disperse or arrest any black person they felt was out of line with the brutal segregated system in Rochester."

Freddie held numerous discussions with Rochester City Council's ranking Republican Frank Horton to try to influence him to end the practice of using K-9 dogs to intimidate young black people. A resolve was found in some incidences, but it still happened.

"It was the typical strategy of municipalities to use the

police and the powers of the courts, to subdue legitimate protest and organizations that represented the interest of black people," Bibby said. "In the early 1960s, if you dreamed of a black president, you better wake up and apologize."

The police force in Rochester at any minute could impose their 'Will' on the black community based on the way the wards were concentrated with all the blacks in two places: Corn Hill and the Joseph Avenue area, where most of them are today.

An officer's questionable use of force to subdue a black teenager at a party in the Seventh Ward ignited the 1964 Rebellion.

The uprising happened on July 24, which was just twenty-two days after the Civil Rights Act of 1964. The highly contested legislation outlawed discrimination based on race or color.

"Kids participating in the rebellion would come by and check to see if we were okay and then they would go about and do whatever they were doing," Midge said. "We knew some of them belong to gangs. One of the boys went to the library to look for instructions on how to make an explosive. He couldn't find the instructions, so he asked the receptionist for help. Freddie scolded him for thinking about making dynamite. And furthermore for being so dumb to ask the receptionist to help him look for the instructions."

Freddie reversed the philosophy of gangs to something positive. He changed their philosophy from something constructively bad, to something constructively good. Another experience that points to his positive influence on gangs was inspiring members to raise money to buy a color television for James and Bessie Hamm. The Hamms' were a senior couple dedicated to community activism.

One of many of their roles as community activists were as facilitators for the Ralph Bunche Scholarship.

Bunche, an African American political scientist and diplomat received the 1950 Nobel Peace Prize for his late 1940s' mediations in Palestine. The path to college for many of the students Freddie tutored depended on the Bunche Scholarships that were provided by the Hamms.

"He would grab kids that weren't supposed to make it. And then one day you see them again with a cap and gown on graduating from some university," New York Assembly member David Gantt said.

Freddie transformed a street gang that called themselves The Soul Brothers. He taught them how to write a proposal for a Community Development Block Grant to open an educational facility on Clarissa Street. The members hired teachers of their choice and taught from a curriculum that included classes in reading, math, English, photography, art and Black History.

"We made sure the kids were prepared for college," said Myron Moxley, former member of The Soul Brothers. "The majority of black kids that graduated from the city schools were not recipients of a quality education. During our days running the community school, Freddie always reminded us that *"Fine schools do not make fine people, but fine people make fine schools."*

The youth Freddie tutored and mentored were organized in different types of clubs that exercised various deeds of goodwill in the community. Unlike the Soul Brothers, the mission was to provide children with a quality education beyond the traditional school model of learning. The Teen Association Club was organized to provide services for senior citizens.

"Freddie didn't want us to just live here in Rochester," Moxley said. "But also participate in making our community better."

In the mid-1960s, Freddie spent an enormous amount of time with youths teaching them everything from basic rudiments of English and mathematics to complex mathematics, physics, philosophy, and religion.

It was his way to seek out young brothers in the streets, get them interested in learning and then teaching them, if they were willing to apply themselves. There's no way of knowing how many people Freddie influenced in this way. And who owe their intellectual curiosity and accomplishment to him.

Knowing the number of people he taught and influenced is near impossible, especially since a primary message of Freddie's teaching was to pass-on the knowledge they had acquired to others.

He tutored all kinds of people in all kinds of places. However, he never had a teaching certificate and never received any financial compensation in return. He didn't do it because he was after any gain of money or power. It was his natural way of living. Freddie was indeed, a *Silent Leader.*

He had such a rapport with young people that a number of those who went on to college, even went so far as to have their college progress reports sent to him rather than to their parents.

"I recall one of his teaching efforts involving a social club of about forty boys and girls," Archie Adams said. "This group approached him and asked,if he would help them learn a few things. Freddie agreed with two conditions. They should rent a place suitable for teaching sessions. And they should construct a chalkboard. The chalkboard was to be constructed from a large piece of cardboard, which was to be framed and painted black.

Freddie would not permit one to be bought to intentionally evoke a lesson in self-reliance. He soon began teaching the students one night out of the week for about a year."

His pioneering work in education and science had garnered national praise and was also being recognized internationally.

In 1967 alone, he had lectured in Sierra Leone, West Africa; Rio de Janeiro, Brazil; Siena and Milan, Italy; Brussels, Belgium; Copenhagen, Denmark and Tokyo, Japan.

The students he tutored and mentored celebrated his nomination to be among the more than 1,000 distinguished scientists that were invited to attend a meeting in Paris,

France for the First International Congress of the
Transplantation Society in 1967.

And they were equally astonished when Freddie received
word from London that he had been nominated for
membership in the Royal Society of Health.

It's one of Britain's most respected societies and largest
group of its kind in the world.

Freddie's independent work in continuous flow dynamics,
perfusion chambers and tissue culture techniques, relating
to historic compatibility concerning transplantation was
transforming the cytology field.

"If you know who you are then you will realize whose shoulders we are standing on and recognize that our responsibility always demands excellence in whatever we do"-Dr. Freddie Thomas

After the 1964 Rebellion, officials at city hall made a commitment to hire more minorities. But executives of big industries like Kodak were not on board. The companies were vowed to not hire or train black workers with blue-collar skills for positions other than as custodians.

It was rumored that Kodak funded a private investigation to obtain a list that contained the names of people arrested in the rebellion. The majority was from Florida, Georgia, South Carolina and parts of Alabama. And supposedly the investigation had also revealed that representatives of the United States Government elected in southern states were not lobbying for large manufacturing industries like Kodak and Xerox to build factories in their states.

After the rebellion, manufacturing industries in Rochester for the first time began lobbying southern politicians to build factories in their states, as an option to stop the migration from the south.

The investigative report concluded with information that

alluded to a fixed position that the efforts of the companies to build factories in southern states failed. The tangible evidence to that conclusion is the continuous protests in the streets leading to Kodak's administrative offices with people holding signs saying, '*Kodak Snaps the Shutter on Negroes.*'

A strategy to unite the dissidents into a political force was formulated by Minister Franklin Florence, former Pastor of Reynolds Street Church of Christ.

Florence decided to invite Saul Alinsky, a political activist from Chicago, Illinois to help organize the movement.

Freddie advised Minster Florence in closed meetings. Florence relied on Freddie's knowledge and experience as a social activist.

"Freddie believed very strongly that we couldn't do anything unless we come together," Constance Mitchell said. "The community was too fragmented at the time, which it still is."

Inspired by the biblical phrase, '*Fight the good fight of faith, lay hold on eternal light,*' the anti-segregation voice of the black community in Rochester was organized under the name FIGHT (Freedom, Integration, God, Honor, Today) in June 1965.

Several white churches in Rochester united to support the demands of FIGHT, by forming an organization called *Friends of FIGHT.*

After a 2-year struggle with the FIGHT organization, Kodak agreed to create a program that will train and employ more than 700 minorities, over an 8-month span.

As a social-political organization the opportunities to employ minorities were limited. Therefore, the FIGHT organization had to morphed into a small manufacturing firm in 1967 and re emerged as FIGHTON (now Eltrex Industries) to meet requirements.

The new company demanded equitable consideration and awarding of contracts from the city of Rochester and firms, including Kodak, Xerox and Bausch & Lomb.

Florence lost the presidency of FIGHT in 1969 to Freddie's mentee, Bernard Gifford.

Gifford, a postgraduate student at the University of Rochester was studying for a doctorate in Radiation Biology and Biophysics at the U of R.

"In the 1960s we were just starting to understand the genetic code of humans," Gifford said. "It was the early period of the biol-geneticrevolution. Blacks in the research department were rare. I think Freddie was the only one.

Freddie didn't apologize for being black. And during the late 1960s into the 1970s it was important to have a senior black man as a role model."

Gifford was active in black affairs on campus as a member of the Black Student Union. It was not until the late 1960s did the university saw the need for a deliberate policy for the recruitment of minority students.

The first ten years produced modest results, although there were signs of administrative effort and faculty support.

In 1981 the University recruited Gifford to return to the U of R as a high-ranking officer for student affairs. The new vice president was brought aboard to provide significant leadership for the university's initiatives in minority affairs.

A study conducted by the University called, '*Report of the Residential College Subcommittee on Diversity*' stated that, "Gifford exercised leadership in several key areas by recruiting additional minority staff as when he appointed Marion Walker, an African American University of Rochester alumnus from the class of 1974, to a new position as director of Minority Affairs. And carefully studied minority student academic performance and designed a '*Minority Peer Counseling Program,*' to help students make the academic and social adjustments necessary for success at the university," the study reported.

"Gifford also worked with admissions to create a Frederick Douglass Scholar Program (deliberately parallel to the Joseph C. Wilson Scholar Program) to target a select group of high performance minority students."

Gifford asserts that much of his push for diversity at predominantly white educational institutions was inspired by conversations he shared with Freddie. He helped many of us understand that everyone including whites should have the opportunity to learn and research how important people of color were to the development of human society.

"Freddie was impressive, articulate and at key moments very resourceful," Gifford said. "He had powerful contacts with a myriad of people, of different ethnicities, political persuasions and religious backgrounds."

One key long-standing working relationship he shared was with Georgiana Harper Sibley.

The Sibley a wealthy white family has been a leading voice in Rochester's social and political affairs, during the city's years of infancy.

Georgiana spent the greater portion of her life promoting the principles of egalitarianism, especially in Rochester.

Her activities of promoting racial justice, ecumenism and educational objectives are monumental.

She was highly respected in the white and black community and often served as a mediator between the two.

Georgina's husband, the grandson of Hiram Sibley was the Director of Western Union. A company his grandfather found, as well as numerous banks and other corporations. Harper Sibley also served as the president of the United States Chamber of Commerce.

As president of Church Women United, Georgiana partnered with local black churches, including A.M.E. Zion and Mt. Olivet Baptist, to break down racial and social barriers in Rochester.

Ethel Banks (far left) and Georgiana Harper Sibley (far right) at Second
Baptist Church, Mumford, NY (November 1966)

Georgiana Harper Sibley (second left) and Ethel Banks (second right)

Rochester's Democrat and Chronicle reported in 1967 that Georgiana's son, Harper Jr., tells of receiving a phone call from a city official urging him to cut his business trip short to come back to Rochester and stop his mother from bailing out black people after they had been arrested during the 1964 Rebellion.

When the office of President of Rochester Area Council of Churches became vacant in 1966 over an internal dispute whether to support FIGHT. At 79 years old, Georgiana accepted the position. Georgiana was firm in her belief that,

"Equality is not an anthropological, political, sociological, or economic question; it is a theological question. Either God made everybody in his own image, or he didn't make anybody at all."

Georgiana goal was to make Rochester, the first fully integrated city in the country.

Besides integration, she also encouraged black people to develop '*pride,*' which correlates with the essential component of Freddie's philosophy.

Furthermore, Georgiana entrusted millions of dollars to a local Presbyterian Church to support causes that challenges racial inequality in Rochester.

After the 1964 Rebellion, the money made it possible for Earl Washington to secure bond insurance for a multimillion-dollar painting project sponsored by the United States Department of Housing and Urban Development.

"Freddie selected my board of directors and spent two days prepping me on how to respond to specific questions before arranging a meeting with the Presbyterian Church," Washington said. "It was a vicious cycle. But at the end of the day, I was signing documents that secured my company the required bond insurance for one of the largest painting contracts in the state of New York."

The rebellion destroyed properties mostly in black communities. But it got the attention of local public officials. Suddenly and unexpectedly, minorities were finding opportunities in fields that were off limits before the uprising.

Herb Hamlett, a former speechwriter for former Senator Robert F. Kennedy was hired by WCMF-FM, a local radio station in Rochester in 1968.

Hamlett was the first full-time black radio disc jockey in Rochester and one of the first Afro Americans in the country to introduce, the FM dial oppose-to-AM radio dial frequency.

"They wouldn't give me advertising dollars," Hamlett said. "And cars at the time didn't come equipped with FM stations, so I had to get in the street myself and advertise. Freddie advice to me was to get off the air, if you're not telling them the truth. I was successful and because of Freddie I was able to stay grounded."

The radio show included community news and provided an outlet for leaders to engage with the black community.

Freddie, a regular guest on the show provided black history questions for listeners that sent them running to the closest library to find the answers.

Despite consecutive years of success, the station hired a new general manager in 1971 to put together a buyout of stockholders and create a 24-hour underground rock platform.

Hamlett was forced out. So, Freddie advised him to explore telecommunications, a relatively new field with a revolutionary future.

After taking classes in the field, Hamlett landed a job at telecom giant IT&T, before moving to Atlanta, Georgia after three years at the company to establish the first black-owned telephone company in the United States.

"We all have fancy degrees on the wall," Hamlett said. "But we all got our education from Freddie."

"You don't have to constantly beg someone to get off your back. You only need to stand upright. It is impossible for someone to stand on you when you are not in a prone position"-Dr. Freddie Thomas

Freddie steered Jeron Rogers and many others to James and Bessie Hamms' house on Adams Street, where many of them received Ralph Bunch Scholarships.

Rogers initially went to Grambling State University, before transferring to the University of Buffalo and finally to the University of Texas.

Freddie encouraged his students to attend colleges outside of Rochester with expectations, the foreign environments would allow them to grow independent of the support of their family and friends and become responsible adults.

During the mid-1960s and well into the 1970s, predominantly white colleges had established a number of institutional changes surrounding its school's curriculum.

Those colleges and universities were establishing black studies programs and departments to attract minorities to their institutions.

Colgate Rochester Crozer Divinity School hired its first

full-time African American professor, Dr. John David Cato, to teach a course related to Black History in 1968.

In June of 1969, the program of Black Church Studies was added to the school's curriculum. Within that program, there were five African American professors and one adjunct professor that began teaching black and white students from a course listing of eight subjects.

"I sought spiritual food freely from Freddie and to this day I am indebted to him for many of the insights I now have," Dr. Cato said.

It was a tribute to Freddie's lifelong efforts when predominantly white institutions added to their curriculum courses to show that black people played a pivotal role in the cultural, intellectual and material development of human society.

Freddie was contacted by several colleges for help in establishing black studies programs within their institutions. And many of the colleges and universities requests came with an opportunity to counsel students.

As a college counselor at Buffalo State College, Freddie was able to create an opportunity for kids to advance their learning.

"I dropped out of high school and went in the military,"

said William Lewis, former city school principal. "When I returned to Rochester, I worked for Kodak for six years."

Lewis was dissatisfied with his job at Kodak. So Freddie advised him to submit an application to attend Buffalo State College.

Lewis said after filling out the application, Freddie told him all he had to do was show up and he'll handle the rest. And after two weeks, he was taking classes. And in less than ten years, he had gone from that position to become the principal at School #58 for 28 years.

In the last meeting of Monroe Community College's, *'All College Committee'* in 1970, a suggestion was made to have a person experienced and well known in the field of black studies answer questions and advise the committee concerning what could be done towards getting a black studies program at the college.

Freddie's reputation was well known among students at the college. So members of a committee that consisted of Tom Price and Bill Benet requested that Freddie come aboard as a consultant.

The meeting was held in the boardroom of Dr. Good's office on the 3rd floor of the administration building at 1000 East Henrietta Road.

Chairperson, James Davis and Board President, Leroy V. Good, attended the meeting. Other attending board members included William Benet, Lucy Mae Jennings, Frank Kinsman, June McClellan, Thomas Price, Charles Speirs and Tony Zito.

According to the minutes from the meeting, Freddie was asked to give his definition of black studies.

Freddie: I considered them to be the same as any other studies concerning any other group of people. Black studies have not been recognized as a discipline. If you don't know black people, you cannot teach them. Often sociology is mistaken for history. They are separate disciplines. Sociology deals with an individual as he relates to another group. Black people have been looked upon as slaves. The history of black people must be studied. You must have an understanding of their history.

Mr. Speirs: Is black studies an assortment of courses that are given at other colleges, which include courses in African History, Afro American History, and Languages, Racial and Ethnic Relations, Problem of Prejudice? And others like Black Writers and so forth?

Freddie: Black history courses are the core of the curriculum. Other courses in the curriculum should be corrected to include black contributions. I suggest, the courses Monroe Community College may offer must be related to the central theme of black culture. Most students have more knowledge of black history than the professor.

Dr. Good: Since Monroe Community College is a two-year college; many of the students will transfer. Considering this, what specific courses should Monroe Community College be teaching for transfer students who wish to build up a major? Or what courses we could teach in the career programs?

Freddie: I suggest a course in black literature and one in black history. But is Monroe Community College ready to accept all the courses that are available? The history course should be titled, *History of the Black Race.* And it should outline important contributions made by Blacks towards the cultural, intellectual and material development of the human society.

"You don't always have to move the man, just move the ground he's standing on"-Dr. Freddie Thomas

In 1971, the Fourth International Congress of Cytology at Grosvenor House, Park Lane, invited Freddie to London, England to speak about his invention called,

"A, Chamber and Perfusion System for General and Specialized In vitro Studies."

The Perfusion System is designed to make test tube studies easier, by providing a controlled atmosphere to sustain and identify human cells.

The functional capacity of the system is engineered to map the genetic code of humans. The apparatus and method have permitted successful growth in various chemically defined media of cultures from human thyroid, Hela, mouse lymphoma, Walker and L-cells.

Universities and research institutes from the United States and around the world requested copies of Freddie's work, after an article describing his invention appeared in the Texas Reports Biology Medical Journal (Volume 24. No. 4: 712-719 winter, 1966)

Department of Parasitology
School of Veterinary Medicine
University of Pennsylvania

3800 Spruce Street
Philadelphia, Pa. 19104

Dear Sir:
I would greatly appreciate a reprint of your article entitled
A Chamber and Perfusion System for General
and Specialized in Vitro Studies.

which appeared in Texas Reports Biol. Med. 24,271,700
Thank you.
Sincerely,
1966

DEPARTMENT OF FORESTRY – MINISTÈRE DES FORÊTS
AND — ET DU
RURAL DEVELOPMENT — DÉVELOPPEMENT RURAL

If a reprint is available, I would appreciate receiving
it too in compensation our disponible l'appréciera receiving
A copy of A Chamber and Perfusion System for General
the copy and Specialized In Vitro Studies: Biaxially
Oriented Polystyrene: An Inert Substrate
and Diffusion Membrane For Use in Tissue
Culture.
Published in Tex. Reports Biol. Med., Vol. 24, No. 4
712-19, Winter, 1966.
Yours sincerely,

LIPID RESEARCH LABORATORY
AKRON CITY HOSPITAL
AKRON, OHIO 44309

Dear Doctor: Date: 6-27-67
I would greatly appreciate a reprint of your article
Part. II. Biaxially oriented polystyrene: An inert substrate
and diffusion membrane for use in tissue culture.
Appearing in Texas Reports on Biology & Medicine 24: 712,
Thank you for this kindness.   1966.
Sincerely,
R.A. NEWMAN
M.A.I. Newman, Ph.D.

University of Washington School of Medicine
Department of Obstetrics & Gynecology
Seattle, Washington 98105

Dear Doctor Thomas
I would greatly appreciate a reprint of your article entitled:
A chamber and Perfusion System for general and specially
in vitro studies
Texas Reports in Biol. & Med. Vol. 24 P. 700 1966
If a reprint is not available, please return the data mentioned
above to assist me in locating the article for photocopies.
Thank you.
Sincerely,
Dr Dugan, M.D

SCHOOL OF VETERINARY MEDICINE
UNIVERSITY OF CALIFORNIA
DAVIS, CALIFORNIA

Will you please send me reprints of your articles entitled A
chamber and perfusion system for general and
specialized in vitro studies I & II published in
Texas Rpts Biol Med 1966 Winter
Thank you.
Marlene Moskinen

MEDICAL RESEARCH COUNCIL
DEMYELINATING DISEASES RESEARCH UNIT
11 FRAMLINGTON PLACE,
NEWCASTLE UPON TYNE, 2
ENGLAND

27th April 1967
Dear Dr. Thomas
I should be most grateful if you would kindly send me a
reprint of your paper A Chamber and perfusion
system for general and specialized in vitro
studies Parts I and II
which appeared in Tex. Rep. Biol. Med. 24, 700-719.
With many thanks, I am,
Yours sincerely,
E. J. FIELD,
Honorary Director.

WESTERN RESERVE UNIVERSITY
Department of Preventive Medicine
Cleveland, Ohio 44106

Dear Sir:
If available, I would appreciate a reprint of your
article entitled: A chamber and perfusion system
for general and specialized in vitro studies
Parts I and II
appearing in Texas Reports Biol. Med. 24: 700 and 712, 1966.
Sincerely yours,
A. R. P. B. LARKE
R. P. B. LARKE

Dear Doctor Thomas.
I would appreciate a reprint of your paper which
appeared in Texas Rep. Biol. & Med. 24:700 (1966)
A Chamber and Perfusion System for
general + Specialized in vitro studies Pat I
Thank You.   V. Saini
Department of Biochemistry,
Dalhousie University
Halifax, CANADA

ONTARIO VETERINARY COLLEGE
GUELPH - CANADA

Dear Sir:
If available for distribution, I should appreciate receiving
Texas Rep. Biol. Med. 24, 700
24, 712
Thank you.
R. Smith
DEPT. OF BOTANY
BERKELEY, CALIFORNIA
BERKELEY, CALIFORNIA
94720
4/14/67

Dear Dr. Thomas
Please send me a reprint of your article,
"a chamber and perfusion system for
general and specialized in vitro studies,"
which appeared recently in Texas
Reports in Biology and Medicine.
Thank you.
Sincerely yours,
R. O. Ryan

4 München 23, den 8. III. 67.

Sehr geehrter Herr Kollege
Dear Sir
Monsieur et très honoré collègue,

Für die Übersendung eines Sonderdruckes Ihrer Arbeit:
We should greatly appreciate a reprint of your article:
Nous vous serions très obligé de nous envoyer un tirage à part de votre article intitulé:

A Chamber and Perfusion System for general and
Specialised in Vitro Studies Part I
Texas Reports on Biol. and Med. 4/700, 1966
wären wir Ihnen sehr dankbar. Mit den erprobenten kollegialen Empfehlungen
Sincerely
Avec nos remerciements et l'expression de nos sentiments les meilleurs

H. Holl

PUBLIC HEALTH LABORATORY,
ONTARIO DEPARTMENT OF HEALTH
Box 9000, Postal Terminal A,
Toronto 1, Ontario, Canada.

Dear Sir:
We would be pleased to receive a reprint of your

article in _____

published in _____

Vol. _____ Page ___ Date ____
____ 24 Yours truly, DR. N. A. LABZOFFSKY
Virus Section

UNIVERSITY COLLEGE LONDON

79

DEPARTMENT OF ANATOMY

EUSton: 7050   GOWER STREET WC1

16th March 1967.

I shall be grateful if you will send me the following reprint(s):-
A chamber & perfusion system for general & specialised in
vitro studies. Part I. Biaxially oriented polystyrene :
An inert substance & diffusion membrane for use in tissue
culture. Part II.
Tex.Rep. on Biol. & Med. 24 (1966).

D. W. JAMES

DEPARTMENT OF MICROBIOLOGY
The University of Alberta
Edmonton, Canada

Dear Dr. F. Thomas
I should greatly appreciate receiving a reprint, if available, of
your paper entitled:

A Chamber and Perfusion System for
In Vitro Studies

which appeared in Tex. Rep. Biol. Med. 24(4): 700(1966)

Yours sincerely,
R. G. MARUSYK

Dear Doctor Thomas

I would appreciate a reprint of your article A Chamber &
Perfusion System for general & spec-
ialised studies

which appeared in Tex. Reports Biol. Med.,
vol. 24, No. 4, 700-711; Winter, 1966.

Thank you for your kindness.

Philip J. Hoadly,
Mason Research Institute
31 _____ Howard Street
Worcester 9, Massachusetts _____

UNIVERSITÉ
FACULTÉ DE MÉDECINE
DE STRASBOURG
Service de Chirurgie Biologique
Directeur: Prof. P. MANDEL

Strasbourg, le 15 Mars 1967

Cher Monsieur,
Dear Sir,

Je vous serais reconnaissant de bien vouloir m'envoyer votre tiré à part:
I should be glad if you would send me a reprint of your paper

Texas Reports on Biology and Medicine
vol. 24, 700 et 712, (1966)

et d'autres publications concernant le même sujet.
and of any papers of similar nature.

Meilleurs remerciements, Dr. M. SENSENBRENNER
Yours sincerely,
H. _____

LARS OLSON
DEPARTMENT OF HISTOLOGY,
KAROLINSKA INSTITUTET
STOCKHOLM 60, SWEDEN

Dear Dr. Thomas

I would very much appreciate a reprint of your paper:
A Chamber and Perfusion System
for General   Part I
published in Texas Reports on Biology
and Medicine, v. 24, p.700, 1966
Thanking you in advance, I am

Sincerely yours,
Lars Olson

Frankfurt/Main (Germany)
Ludwig-Rehn-Straße 14 · Theodor-Stern-Haus

Sehr geehrter Herr Professor!
Dear Sir;
Monsieur le Professeur,

Für die Übersendung eines Sonderdruckes Ihrer Arbeit:
I would greatly appreciate a reprint of your article:
et vous serais très obligé de m'envoyer un tirage à part de votre article intitulé:

Texas Rep. Biol. 24, 700 + 712 (1966)

wäre ich Ihnen sehr dankbar. Mit freundlichen Grüßen!
Sincerely yours
Je vous en remercie par avance et vous prie de croire, Monsieur le Professeur, à l'expression de mes
sentiments les plus distingués

Harald Fister

Milano 20th March, 1967

A Chamber and Perfusion System......

Texas Rep. Biol. Med., 24(4), 700, 1966

Sehr geehrter Herr
Dear Dr.
Monsieur et très honoré collègue

Für die Übersendung eines Sonderdruckes Ihrer Arbeit
I would greatly appreciate a reprint of your article
Je vous serais très obligé de m'envoyer un tirage à part de votre article intitulé

wäre ich Ihnen sehr dankbar. Ihr ergebener
Sincerely yours
Je vous en remercie par avance et vous prie de croire,
Monsieur, à mes sentiments les plus distingués

THE CITY OF STOCKHOLM
BLOOD TRANSFUSION CENTRE
SÖDERSJUKHUSET, STOCKHOLM 38, SWEDEN

Date: 7.2.1967

Dear DR P L X TEXAS
I would greatly appreciate receiving a reprint of your article
together with DR I N CLUSE
A chamber and perfusion system for general and
entitled specialized in vitro studies. Part I.
which appeared in Texas Reports on Biology and Medicine
Vol. 24, Winter 1966, No. 4
as well as other available documentation on your work in this field

Thank you for your kindness.

Yours sincerely

Dear Sir,

I would greatly appreciate if you could let me have reprints of your
paper(s) on A Chamber and Perfusion system for general and
specialized in vitro studies. Part I.
Part II. Biaxially oriented polystyrene: An inert
Substrate and Diffusion membrane for use in tissue
Culture.

Texas Reports on Biology and Med., Vol.24: 700,24,1966

and other papers on related subjects, if available for distribution.

Faithfully Yours

Bratislava   5.4.1967.

Sehr geehrter Herr
Dear Sir
Monsieur et très honoré collègue

Je vous serais très obligé de m'envoyer un tirage à part de votre article intitulé;
I would greatly appreciate a reprint of your article.
Für die Übersendung eines Sonderdruckes Ihrer Arbeit;
A chamber and perfusion system for general and specialized
in vitro studies. Part I.
Texas Reports on Biology & Medicine v.24,win.1966,n°4,p.700
Je vous en remercie par avance et vous prie de croire, Monsieur, à mes sentiments les plus distingués.
Sincerely yours.
wäre ich Ihnen sehr dankbar. Mit vollkommen Grüssen!

NATIONAL INSTITUTE FOR MEDICAL RESEARCH
(Medical Research Council)

Tel: 01-959 3666   London N.W.7.

Dear Dr. Thomas:
I should be very grateful if you would send me a
reprint of your paper on:
A chamber + perfusion system for general and
specialized in vitro studies

which appeared in:
Texas Rep. Biol Med 24 700-24
24 712-719

if copies are still available.

Thankyou.

Yours sincerely (P. Teage)

CANCER RESEARCH INSTITUTE
RADIUMSTATIONEN
AARHUS C. DENMARK

DANISH CANCER SOCIETY

Dear Dr. Thomas

I should greatly appreciate receiving a reprint of A Chamber and
Perfusion System for General and Specialized in Vitro Studies
Part I. and Part II. Biaxially Oriented Polystyrene: An Inert
Substrate and Diffusion Membrane for Use in Tissue
Culture   which appeared in

Texas Reports on Biology and Medicine 1966, 24: 700-712
and 712-720.

Sincerely yours

Niels Jacobsen

MEMORIAL HOSPITAL
444 EAST 68 STREET
NEW YORK, NEW YORK 10021

April 7, 1967

I would appreciate a reprint of your article entitled A Chamber & perfusion System for general + specialized in vitro studies etc.

which appeared in Tex. Reports Biol. Med.

Vol. 34 Pages 717-714 Year 1966

Thank you for your courtesy.

Dr. D. Armstrong
Dept.

Dept. of Physiology.

ONTARIO VETERINARY COLLEGE
GUELPH - CANADA

Dear Sir:

If available for distribution, I should appreciate receiving

A Chamber and Perfusion System for General and Specialized in Vitro Studies. Part 1.
Texas Reports on Biology and Medicine 24: 700, (1966).

Thank you.

Dr. A. Noyan.

Department of Physiology
School of Veterinary Medicine
University of Pennsylvania

3800 Spruce Street
Philadelphia, Pa. 19104

Dear Sir:

I would greatly appreciate a reprint of your article entitled

Part II Heavily Oriented Polystyrene
Onboard Sidesteal and Diffusion Membrane for the in Tissue Culture

which appeared in Texas Reports Biol Med 24 (47): 712, 1966

Thank you

Sincerely,
J. A. Novotny

CLARK UNIVERSITY - DEPARTMENT OF BIOLOGY 39
Worcester, Mass., 01610 U.S.A.

Dear Sir:

I would very much appreciate receiving a reprint of your article entitled:

A Chamber and Perfusion System for General and Specialized in Vitro Studies Part I.

which appeared in: Texas Reports on Biology and Medicine Vol 24, Winter 1966, #4, p. 700.

Sincerely,
Dr. D. G. Moulton

THE NEW YORK HOSPITAL-CORNELL UNIVERSITY MEDICAL COLLEGE
525 East 68th Street
New York, N. Y. 10021

I should greatly appreciate receiving a reprint

of your article, A chamber and perfusion system for general and specialized in vitro studies I and II which appeared in

Tex Rep Biol Med 1966, 24: 700, 714.

Sincerely yours,

DEPARTMENT OF PHYSIOLOGY
CORNELL UNIVERSITY MEDICAL COLLEGE
1300 YORK AVENUE, NEW YORK 21, N. Y.

Dear Doctor:

I would greatly appreciate a reprint of your article Chamber & Perfusion System for General & specialized in vitro studies etc etc
appearing in Texas Reports on Biology + Med

24: 700 Winter 1966

Sincerely yours,

Ann Stevens
Neuroendocrine Section
University of New Mexico School of Medicine
2211 Lomas Blvd., N.E.
Albuquerque, New Mexico 87106

MICHIGAN STATE UNIVERSITY
Endocrine Research Unit
Department of Physiology
East Lansing

Dear Sir:

Would you send me a reprint of the paper

A Chamber and Perfusion System for General and Specialized in Vitro Studies. Part I and Part II etc

published in Texas Reports Biol + Med Vol 24 Winter 1966

Thank you and good hunting.
John E. Nellor, Ph. D.

Department of Life Sciences
University of California
Riverside, California

Dear Dr. Thomas

I would appreciate receiving a reprint of your article, entitled

A chamber and perfusion system for general and specialized in vitro studies. Part I, and Part II,

which appeared in Texas Reports... 24(4), Winter 1966, p. 712

Thank you for your courtesy.

Sincerely,
Richard L. Moretti

March 7

UNIVERSITY OF CALIFORNIA MEDICAL CENTER
CANCER RESEARCH INSTITUTE
San Francisco, California 94122

Dear Dr. Thomas
I would appreciate receiving a reprint of your article

Chamber - perfusion system - in vitro studies I + II

Published in: Texas Rept. Biol + Med. 24 pp 700-711, 1966

Thank you for this courtesy.

Della Cochran

U.S.P.H.S. HOSPITAL
1131 14th Avenue South
Seattle, Washington 98144

Dear Doctor Thomas
I would greatly appreciate a reprint of your article
A chamber and perfusion system for general and specialized in vitro studies. Part I

Journal Texas Reports on Biology and Medicine Year Winter 1966

Volume 24 Page 700

Sincerely yours,

UNIVERSITY OF WASHINGTON
DEPARTMENT OF MEDICINE

Baakon Ragde, M. D.

AIR MAIL

Sehr verehrter Herr (Frau) Kollege(in)!
Peat Doctor!

Darf ich Sie bitten, mir einen Sonderdruck Ihrer Arbeit
I would greatly appreciate a reprint of your paper

und damit zusammenhängender Arbeiten zu senden!
and of others on the same subject.

Mit bestem Dank im voraus!
Thank you in advance for your courtesy!

Ihr sehr ergebener
Very truly yours,

DEPARTMENT OF BACTERIOLOGY   17
Dalhousie University, Halifax. N. S.
CANADA

Dear Sir:

I would greatly appreciate a reprint of your article entitled

which appeared in

Yours sincerely,
J.A. EMBIL M.D.

Dear Dr. Thomas,

I would appreciate receiving reprint(s) of your article(s)
on

which appeared in

Sincerely yours,

M. SPAIN
Department of Biology and
McCollum-Pratt Institute
Johns Hopkins University

Dept. of Animal Husbandry
University of California
Davis, California, 95616

Dear Dr. Thomas:

If available, I would appreciate a reprint of your paper(s) entitled
A chamber and perfusion system for general and
specialized in vitro studies Parts I and II

which appeared in Texas Rep. Biol. Med. 24: 700, 712, 1966

Thank you.
J. R. Boda

Department of Microbiology
Oregon State University
Corvallis, Oregon 97331

Dear Colleague:

I would appreciate receiving a reprint of your
article entitled

that appeared in

Thank you,

Sincerely yours,
KARL T. KLEEMAN

DEPARTMENT OF FORESTRY - MINISTÈRE DES FORÊTS
AND   ET DU
RURAL DEVELOPMENT   DÉVELOPPEMENT RURAL

If a reprint is available, I would appreciate receiving a

A copy of   A Chamber and Perfusion System For
the same   General and Specialized In Vitro
Studies.

Published in Tex. Reports Biol. Med., Vol. 24, No. 4:
700-711; Winter, 1966.

Yours sincerely,

WORCESTER FOUNDATION FOR EXPERIMENTAL BIOLOGY   16
— 222 MAPLE AVENUE, SHREWSBURY, MASSACHUSETTS

Dear Doctor:

If reprints of your article entitled A Chamber and Perfusion System

for General and Specialized in Vitro Studies

are available I shall appreciate receiving a copy.

This appeared in Texas Reports on Biol. Med. 24; 700 Winter
1966

Thank you
Delphine Bartosek

GROUPE DE BIOLOGIE CELLULAIRE
INSTITUT DE RECHERCHES SCIENTIFIQUES SUR LE CANCER
BOITE POSTALE Nº 8 · 94·VILLEJUIF · FRANCE

19

DEAR SIR :

If available, we should greatly appreciate
a reprint of your paper which appeared in :
Texas Rep. Biol. Med., 1966, 24; 700-712
: 712-719
A chamber & Perfusion system for general & specialized in vitro studies. I, a biaxially oriented
polystyrene: an inert membrane, a diffusion membrane for use in tissue culture. II,

Very sincerely yours,

DOCTEUR Henri FEBVRE

UNIVERSITY OF CALIFORNIA MEDICAL CENTER

Dear:

I have read with interest your above report. If reprints are
available, I would greatly appreciate a copy for my files.

Sincerely yours,
James B. Smith

Aging Res. Lab.
Baltimore, Md. 21224

Dear Doctor:

I would appreciate receiving a reprint of your
paper entitled, A chamber and perfusion system
which appeared in Texas Reports Biol. and Med. 24 (4)
700-711 & 712-719, 1966.

Thanking you,
R. J. Han Ph.D

Mr. Richard G. Burnham
19 Merrill Drive
Saxonville, Mass. 01706

Dear Dr. Thomas

I would appreciate
your forwarding a
copy of each:
(Regarding Chamber +
perfusion system)
Tex. Reports Biol. Med.
Vol. 24 no 4; 712-719
Winter - 1966
and IBID. 700-711
thank you
R. G. Burnham

R. G. Brackett, Ph.D
Microbiology Department
Parke Davis & Co.
P.O. Box 118, G.P.O
Detroit 32, Michigan

WE ARE VERY INTERESTED IN YOUR PAPER ENTITLED: A Chamber and
Perfusion System for General and Specialized in Vitro Studies
in Tex. Repts Biol. Med. 24 700, 717, 1966 Parts I + II
AND WOULD VERY MUCH APPRECIATE RECEIVING A REPRINT.

SINCERELY,
H. M. Bangslinp, Ph.D.

IMPORTANT
PLEASE FORWARD TO THE ATTENTION OF: Life Sciences Division

An analysis of Freddie's invention by the Black History Museum of Philadelphia found that:

The Perfusion System is able to meet the foregoing demands and overcomes the problems of needle instability, peripheral leakage, cover-ship rupture and unreliability of perfusion rotes presently associated with commercially available equipment.

Some of the outstanding advantages of this system are: design flexibility, handling ease, systemic flexibility, internal environment, accessibility for varied testing and modification and finally low cost, an important factor, especially for black universities who find their budgets shrinking when requests are received from their scientific labs.

A system like Freddie's that's capable of supporting dissociated cell cultures without interacting with the cells is the most important function in the field of cytology.

In the past, the use of glass has been almost exclusive. There are several arguments against the use of glass in this highly sensitive operation:

(1) It's easy to break.

(2) It has the tendency to produce strong cell to glass attachment.

(3) It's varied and possibly toxic make-up is limiting.

Therefore, Freddie and his associate Lester Cramer proposed the use of a plastic material called polystyrene. The trade name of the product is Polyflex and commonly supplied as film and sheet. It's crisp, not affected by moisture of humidity and will not soften, wrinkle or shrink in water.

Freddie's experiments using Polyflex have solved several major problems when working with cell structures.

The Black History Museum Committee presented Freddie with the '*Imhotep Ernest E. Just Scientific Award*,' for scholarly excellence pioneering studies in Black History and Cytology, blacks in the medical field and numerous other scientific works."

Beyond the international clamor to have him come to London, Freddie decided he wasn't going to attend the International Congress of Cytology at Grosvenor House, Park Lane. By Freddie's measure, the financial cost for a five-day stay was too expensive. So his students organized numerous fundraisers to cover the cost of the trip.

Midge remembered, when Freddie returned from London. She gave him a hug when he got off the plane and noticed he had lost somewhere around ten pounds. And his response was that he limited himself to eating one meal a day so he could buy some books in England.

The inside covers of the books were encrypted with the words, '*Not to be sold in the United States.* The books documented the history of blacks in Africa and the early civilizations of Africans in Asia.

Shortly after returning, Freddie received a letter from the United Nations that requested his participation in the African Student Exchange Program.

The program provides opportunities for African students to enroll in graduate programs all over the world. Housing the exchange students at the homes of black families was a step away from the norm, when the Thomases' were assigned their first student. Wealthy white families traditionally sponsored the exchange students designated to study in Western New York.

Before Freddie's involvement in the program, many of the exchange students were unaware of Rochester's black community. The colorful dashikis worn by the African exchange students became a fashion trend for local youths. The garment's popularity inspired Gene Lockhart and Joan Howard Coles, to open a store that sold Dashikis and other African cultural arts and crafts. It was one of the first black stores to open its doors in Midtown Plaza.

"Blacks and whites shopped at our store because it was very different," Joan said. "The dashikis and other merchandise we carried were limited designs. A lot of what we sold came directly from Africa and some I did myself." The store was incorporated under the name *Uhuru*, a Swahili word meaning Freedom.

"The name is a testament to our ancestral consciousness that Freddie helped us to transform into a business," Joan said.

African diplomats visiting the United States often stayed at the Thomases' home.

Freddie was able to initiate dialogue with people of all different ethnicities and persuasions. He could hold a conversation with a gang member or in another instance, a well-educated diplomat. Both conversations for him would be natural and genuine.

Some of the African diplomats compared their conversations with Freddie to those they've had with their grandfathers. They were fascinated with Freddie's broad composite of knowledge on African History and Culture.

Ahmed Saray-Warie, an African exchange student sponsored by the Thomases' was from Freetown, Sierra

Leone. He was studying for a doctorate in Sociology at Lincoln University in Pennsylvania.

Ahmed is unfortunately remembered for erasing a composition written by Freddie about Anne Frank that was logged on a cassette recorder. Anne Frank, an adolescent of Jewish descent died in a Nazi-Germany concentration camp in 1945, at the age of 15.

Ahmed was fascinated that, the cassette recorder could play back his voice. He called the recorder, a talking box. He unintentionally erased the pre-recorded content on the cassette, by continuing to record his voice over and over. The loss of the recording was unfortunate for Freddie knowing that he couldn't duplicate the final version that was on the cassette after spending hours on the piano perfecting the song.

Freddie, Dunbar, and Me

"Mrs. Thelma Philips wanted me to do some poetry written by *Dunbar*," Sylvia Barker said. "I refuse to do it and planned to show up sick. Then Freddie got the book out and started to recite. I was shocked into amazement. I could not believe my ears. How beautiful the poems sounded, the way Freddie read them."

Then Freddie said, "*now you do it, and make us very proud.*"

"I took the book for one week and started practicing. The poems by Dunbar made me famous. I've performed now for seventeen years with Midge and Freddie clapping in the audience."

-Paul Laurence Dunbar (1872-1906) was a famous African American poet, novelist and playwright of the late nineteenth and twentieth centuries.

Dr. Thomas presenting Sylvia Barker with an award for poetry and storytelling (1965)

"We are a new people. We have been transformed into people like no one has seen before"-Dr. Freddie Thomas

Freddie flew out to Monterey, California to speak at a Symposium on microwave power after returning from England in 1971.

His worldwide popularity as a leading figure in education and science, kept him busy. While packing a suitcase for a conference in Chicago, he felt a sharp pain in his abdomen.

After taking a painkiller, he decided to postpone a trip to the doctor so he could attend the symposium. When he returned, his physician gave him a laxative to examine his digestive organs.

Freddie took purgatives every day for a week, until they found a black spot on the eleventh vertebrate of his spine. However, they were unable to specify whether he had either cancer or tuberculosis.

Following weeks of blood work in September of 1972, he was diagnosed with having multiple myeloma, a cancer that starts in the plasma cells in bone marrow.

Bone marrow is the soft, spongy tissue found inside most bones. It helps make blood cells. Plasma cells help your body fight infection by producing proteins called antibodies. Several medical studies indicate:

"In cases of multiple myeloma, plasma cells grow out of control in the bone marrow and form tumors in the areas of solid bone. The growth of these bone tumors makes it harder for the bone marrow to make healthy blood cells and platelets."

For myeloma risk factors include:

• the disease is more than twice as common in African Americans than is white Americans;

• the risk of myeloma goes up as people age;

• men are more likely to develop myeloma than women;

• having a personal history of the disease or genetic abnormalities;

• being exposed to radiation or certain chemicals in the workplace.

Having any of these risk factors does not mean you will contract the disease because the origin of myeloma is unknown.

Some people who develop myeloma have none of the above risk factors, but Freddie's years as a biochemist does give weight to the suggestions that the progression of the disease could be related to his work.

According to Freddie's former physician, it is possible that being exposed to so much radiation could have contributed or either precipitated his illness.

"The genetic researchers wore red aprons [film badges] that protected your chest and testicles, but it didn't protect you from what might be in the air," Dr. Perry Eck said. "The workers wore a badge that measures the radiation around you. If it went to a certain level, they would pull you out and give you a break, but the badge only measured what it comes across and not the stuff bouncing off the walls. A test could not be run on how it affected humans because it's unethical, so they used animals."

In a report administered by the University of Rochester Department of Radiation Biology and Biophysics:

[Most of the research during World War II and for sometime afterwards was devoted to answering urgent questions raised in atomic energy production facilities on the toxicity of materials and the biological effects of radiation.

Research to provide direct answers to such questions involved exposures of various species of animals in numbers large enough to yield answers of statistical significance.

As a result of this development, very productive investigations of the physiology, biochemistry and structure of bones and teeth evolved from earlier studies of the toxicity of the bone-seeking heavy metals.

Although in studying these problems, the fundamental biological mechanisms involved were not neglected; they were not given principle attention.]

Bone marrow transplants didn't become an option for myeloma patients until 1984, so the disease was incurable.

Dr. Eck treated patients suffering from the illness with Cytoxan and tetra zone, a form of cortisone. And Freddie was prescribed to take 128 pills within four days of each month and ordered to undergo several rounds of chemotherapy.

"Back then, there was no better treatment but if he had it now, I would refer him to a hospital that did bone marrow transplants," Dr. Eck said. "I am sure, if there was something wrong with my treatment, he would tell me. He was a lot brighter than I am. Freddie was employed at Strong Memorial Hospital and I was not and I am sure he made it there on his ability."

Dr. Eck wasn't sure how much time Freddie had to live, but suggest two to three years based on previous cases.

"When I gave him the news, Freddie's character never changed," Dr. Eck said. "He was very calm about it. And I was amazed by how he accepted it. Once back home, his illness didn't slow him down.

In an interview in 1973 with Wagner College Magazine, Freddie said he had always been interested in the welfare of youngsters, but holding down a regular position as a research assistant at the U of R never left him enough time. Now that he was unable to work in the laboratory, he can do what he feels is important.

"I have a lot of work to do," Freddie declares. "I need five-hundred years to do all I want to do, but if I only have a couple of years left to use, well that's all right too. I can make a whole lot of hay in the next two years."

With the free time on his hands, Freddie found and published '*The Evidence Newspaper' and served as editor of 'Rochester Peoples weekly.*'

To compliment the publications, Freddie created '*Original Researchers*, a personalized consultant firm that specializes in research on education, science and mathematics in areas where blacks had made contributions that weren't generally known by the public.

He accepted a visiting lecturer position in Black Studies and Research at Howard University in Washington, D.C. And continued to travel, wherever he gets the call for seminars, workshops and the like.

Some of the lectures were of his professional capacity as a biologist. But the great majority were in the field of Black and African studies. After disassembling all his projects at the laboratory, he brought it home and continued to do research. A collaborative study with his boyhood friend Cecil Rhodes produced a number of breakthroughs on oral cancer at Cecil's dentistry in Norfolk, Virginia.

"We made numerous trips to Norfolk, Virginia so Freddie and Cecil could collaborate and to visit family and friends," Midge said. "If they were kids around the station when we stopped for gas, Freddie would walk up to them and start teaching. He only needed a small stick from the branch of a tree to draw scientific equations and mathematical calculations in the dirt," Midge said. "Freddie could see the beauty in every child, rich or poor. And while traveling back and forth, we would see those boys. And they would run up to him eager to learn something new," she chuckled. "One of the boys asked, if Freddie was God."

Freddie and Midge's trips to conferences up and down the Midwest and eastern coast were priceless times spent together. While in different cities, they would unexpectedly drop-in on friends and former students.

"On several occasions Freddie and his wife came down from Rochester to visit," Archie Adams said. "On one such visit, Freddie and I spent nearly an entire Saturday in downtown Philadelphia searching for old books going from old book store to old book store. I recall, one bookstore owner apparently thought we came in to rob him," Adams said. "He watched us like a hawk before Freddie asked him a few discreet questions about certain rare volumes. The owner then realized where we were coming from. By the end of that afternoon, Freddie had bought a number of old books and was quite elated over his newly acquired possessions."

He didn't converse much about the disease, especially with his students. Freddie viewed death as making a transition to a higher level of existence, where others who had passed away had advanced to continue their life journeys.

"Freddie said to me and two other brothers that he was walking down the street and he ran into an angel," William Lewis said. "So we knew we didn't have much time left with him? Plus he was teaching around the clock, hardly sleeping and was always in the street," Lewis recall.

At the New York State Fair with several students, Freddie directed their attention toward the cows and began to explain how commercial farmers and corporations would take hormones from pregnant cows and use those hormones as feed for the calves.

As a result, those calves will get bigger and grow faster than normal. And they would take that meat, grind it up and packaged it for commercial consumption.

Freddie predicted the unnatural process would produce a nation of obese and unhealthy children from modest economic backgrounds in the years to come.

"They were doing the same process with the chickens," Lewis said. "And hearing those predictions as a kid and living to see them manifest into reality as an adult is at times mind-blowing."

Freddie was adamant on the point that humans should be knowledgeable about their bodies and the environment in which they live or it can be catastrophic. He believed a healthy physical body reflects a healthy mind.

Freddie's commitment to health issues and solutions led to a decision by his student Walter Lee, to study nutrition, which at the time was a rare interest in the black community. He also was deeply involved in Lee's first film on Sickle Cell Anemia.

"Dr. David Satcher, a postgraduate student of the U of R said, he wouldn't have gone on to become United States Surgeon General, if it wasn't for the film Freddie and I produced in 1970," Lee said.

After a lecture on African History at the Rochester Museum and Science Center in 1973, '*The Black Race: Some Contributions to Civilizations*,' Freddie's leg went weak. From that day on, he was paralyzed and never walked again.

My Duty

When I think about my life's dreams I think how simple it
seems. It's so easy to plan the right deeds to help my fellow
man needs

Dr. Freddie Thomas (1933, age 15)

"Freddie was very interested in exploring the history of
humankind and what he found was black people at the top
of the list," Dr. Eck said. "His biological knowledge was
concentrated in genetics, so it was almost destined in a time
when racism was prevalent. Freddie had pertinent
information that he believed could restore self-pride back in
black people from the knowledge he obtained through the
field of genetics. This could be a link to who he was and
why he became who he was," Dr. Eck said.

Most medical journals define a geneticist as a biologist who
studies genetics, the science of genes, heredity, and
variation of organisms. Geneticists can be employed as a
researcher or lecturer. Some geneticists perform
experiments and analyze data to interpret the inheritance of
skills.

A geneticist is also a consultant or medical doctor who has
been trained in genetics as a specialization. They evaluate,

diagnose, and manage patients with hereditary conditions or congenital malformations, genetic risk calculation, and mutation analysis as well as refer patients to other medical specialties.

And they participate in courses from many areas, such as biology, chemistry, physics, microbiology, cell biology, bioinformatics, English, and mathematics."

"During the early years of the 20th century, many Jewish families like my own immigrated to the United States from Belgium," Dr. Eck said. "I earned my medical degree at Albert Einstein College of Medicine in Bronx, New York. And when I returned from serving in the United States military in 1966, I was selected for an internship at Rochester General Hospital to complete my training, before opening a practice at 1157 Fairport Road," he said.

"When Freddie became paralyzed from the waist down, I began treating him at his home on Skuse Street. My trips to the Thomases' home were always at night. And it was a dog across the street from his house trained to eat white people and I don't blame it," Eck chuckles and recall.

"It was barking like crazy from behind the fence and then someone let it out and he was chewing my fender. Luckily, I was in the car. At his home, Freddie insisted the hospital bed be placed in the living room, so he could continue to teach his students."

"As the disease advanced into the bone marrow, Freddie started having pain. When he flexed his muscle it was painful, because myeloma causes the bones to cramp up and to collapse. Also he began suffering from constant weight loss, wasting of muscle and loss of appetite," Dr. Eck said. "He became anemic."

A student from an area college or university would come and sit with him from 4pm to 6pm, someone else would come from 6pm to 8pm, someone else would come from 8pm to 10pm and someone else would come and spend the night. Freddie would be teaching the students and helping to upgrade their marks, while lying down on the bed paralyzed.

"If he wanted a glass of water, despite the fact that he we wanted to be there to make sure he got it," Moxley said. "Midge was worn out and at times he would get terrible cramps in his legs. However he was able to control the pain, despite he was bedridden. I've seen cramps in his leg bigger than a baseball and he would not flinch. Freddie would close his eyes and shift the pain," Moxley said.

Freddie's Alma Mater-Wagner College, rallied around him

as his health gradually deteriorated. Freddie was determined to visit Wagner in person, but the side effects from his prescribed medications made long drives difficult. They could barely reach Ithaca, New York before he felt sick and eventually had to return home.

In a letter to Wagner College Magazine, Freddie writes:

"Just a belated note to the Wagner alumni for the truly wonderful and generous way they responded to my illness. This is my first letter in my own handwriting; I am trying to get my strength. Briefly, I have a "non- curable" disease of the bones, which make certain blood cells, a condition called multiple myeloma. It is painful when the bones themselves ache. Some improvement.....indeed, quite a bit......is noted. I take 128 pills within four days of each month. I am not working now.....on indefinite disability. This has sort of put a crimp in my plans for further study at the University of Rochester for a while. That doctorate plan is shelved. In any case, the enclosed paper and one other is due for publication. I have much I would like to do, but, well.....haven't much time, unless a miracle or a new discovery occurs or is made. The doctor says people have lived for three years. Midge and I tried to make a surprise

appearance for last Homecoming. We got as far as Ithaca,
but my condition forced us to stop and discontinue the trip.
We had hoped to pay our respects in person. Pastor Reissig
came by to see me at the hospital. Their (Ron and his)
coming rekindled the old fires for Wagner College and the
cards! My word, you must have a file on every Wagner
alumnus, living and dead! The cards came and letters came
from everywhere! I don't know how to say, "Thank you" to
them all. I hope someday to write them. My strength is
returning, thanks to Almighty God. The many students
whom I have met come in and out and keep my spirits up. I
sometimes feel I am slowed up in leading them to higher
levels of education as I must rest now and cannot engage
actively in educational advancement on a personal basis.
Maybe, if God so wills, I can get well enough to do enough
advanced study to at least get my doctorate to complete my
life's work, at least! I cannot engage, so it seems formally
in further intensive or serious scientific research as I did
last year. It all seems so strange; I have never been able to
not work before."

Achievement Award presented to Dr. Freddie Thomas by Fred White,
President Wagner College Alumni Association. (1969)

Nature's Eternal Life and Four Seasons

-The Signs of spring: life, babies, youth, cheerful, loving, happiness, and innocence, stimulating, sprouting, shouting, bursting, and lively.

-The Signs of summer: experiencing, learning, exploring, whispering, laughing, running, playing, shining, exciting, stimulating, and loving.

-The Signs of fall: traveling, moving, studying, remembering, reminiscing, shifting gears, slowing down, chilling out, appreciating, loving.

-The Signs of winter: preparation, restful, hiding, loving, peaceful, dead, transfer, transition, completeness, finish, farewell, glorious.

-Dr. Freddie Thomas, February 12, 1974

"One night he said I'm not going to be with you much longer," Midge said. "He spoke about life and death and how we didn't come here to stay because we have to replenish the earth by returning our bodies to the soil. He gave an analogy that was congruent with nature, saying that the spring flowers bloom to die in the fall to replenish the soil for the next spring. He had a way of using nature to explain the nuisances of life. His thoughts on some of the toughest things to talk about were spoken so poetically and romantically," Midge said.

"I needed to have a cassette recorder by my side, when we spoke. But when I asked, could I go retrieve it? He would say, honey this conversation is for you. I think he saw how important it was to me, so the next day he wrote the analogy down calling it, *Nature's Eternal Life and Four Seasons,* " she said. "Throughout his sickness I never grieved and instead we talked about life and death before he died. We had our closure before hand, so my thought about it was pleasurable."

Freddie spent his last few days at the North side Division of Rochester General Hospital. And at this point he was mostly incapacitated and awaiting transition.

He was in and out of consciousness and rambling in a frail voice. And at times he would awake from his medicated slumber and talk about something so intellectually profound the people in the room would be in awe and then he would fall back into a deep sleep.

Paul Jones, a kid he tutored and nurtured was a graduate of the University of Texas with a Bachelor of Science degree in chemical engineering. When Paul was about to graduate from college, his mother gave the plane ticket to Midge as a Testament to her belief that she should be the one to see him accept his degree.

Paul booked a flight to Rochester after hearing Freddie was in his last days.

"When he walked in the hospital room, he broke down and cried," Midge said. "So, I took him outside and told him not to cry in front of Freddie because it was late in his illness. He was so sincere like he was losing his best friend. And shortly after returning to the room, the doctor came to me and said it is time. I told everyone to leave, so I could say good-bye to my husband."

On Sunday, February 24, 1974, Freddie died from profound cachexia, due to multiple myeloma at 9:30a.m. His approximate interval between onset and transition was 2 and a 1/2 years.

"You don't have to worry about the opposition, just raise the bar so high that only the champs can go over. The amateurs will all have to slide underneath it."-Dr. Freddie Thomas

CURRICULUM VITAE

Freddie Levy Thomas

Born:	February 10, 1918, Norfolk, Virginia
Died:	February 24, 1974, Rochester, New York
Married:	Midge Banks, February 9, 1957
Parents:	James Thomas and Hattie Armstrong
Siblings:	Sisters: Muriel, Shirley, Rebecca
	Brothers: Iris and Gene
Education:	B.S. Wagner College, New York
	Albany Medical School (1952)
	University of Rochester (1972)

Experience:

Eastman Kodak Company, Rochester, NY

Research Technologist (1952-1960)

University of Rochester School of Medicine and Dentistry

Rochester, NY

Research Assistant (1961-66)

Research Associate (1966-1972)

Membership Held:

Visiting Lecturer-Howard University

African Studies Research (1972-73)

AAA, Univ. Archaeology. Soc.;

Brigham Young Univ.;

Math Assn. Amer.;

Soc. Photographic Science & Engineers;

Tissue Culture Assoc.;

Assn. Study, Negro Life, History;

Phi Sigma Kappa;

Rochester C of C;

Rochester Academy Sci.;

N.Y. Academy Sci.;

Hist. of Sci. Soc.;

Soc. Amer. Historians, Inc.;

Amer. Assoc. Hist. Med. Inc.;

Sigma Xi;

Soc. Appl Anthropology; Mason, A.F.

Soc. Soc. Cryobiology.;

Pakistan Assn.; Advance Sci.;

Radiation Res. Soc. International Platform Assn.;

Ghana Science Association;

Publisher & Editor:

The Evidence Newspaper;

Former ed.-Rochester Peoples Weekly

Invited Lectures:

Extensively throughout the United States, Canada, and Bermuda and Internationally on African and Afro American History

The 1st International Congress of The Transplantation

Society, Paris, France, (June 26-30, 1967)

Honors:

-Rhodes Scholar Nominee, Wagner College

-Outstanding Achievement Award by Natl. Assn. Negro
Business And Professional Women's Assn., Rochester
chapter

-1964 Parents and Students Want To Know Group Award
for Community service, Rochester, NY (1968)

Areas of Research:

-Cell Biology

-Tissue Culture

-Photographic Science

-African History

-Philosophies of the East (Buddhism, Hinduism, etc.)

Scientific Listings:

-Who's Who in American Education (1965-66; 1966-67)

-Leaders in American Science (Vols. 5, 6, 7, 8)

-Combined Listings of Mathematicians (1966)

-American Men of Science, Physical and Biological
Sciences

-11thEd. (1967) Who's Who in the East 12thEd

-Dictionary of International Biography 5thEd

-Who's Who in Biomedical Engineering, (1967-68)

BIBLIOGRAPHY:

1. Thomas, F. L.: *In Reply to the Question of the Repatriation of the Negro*. The Norfolk Journal and Guide Newspaper, (April 17, 1943)

2. Thomas, F. L.: *History of the African in Asia*, the Empire Star Newspaper Buffalo, N.Y. (June 6, 1957, through December 19, 1958)

3. Thomas, F. L.: *Negro Members of Parliament*. The Empire Star Newspaper Buffalo, N.Y. (1958)

4. Thomas, F.L.: And Cramer, L. M.: *A New Chamber and Perfusion System for General and Specialized in Vitro Studies* (Tissue Culture Assoc. Annual Meet, Abstract Papers) Miami Beach, Florida, (May 31-June 3, 1965, 16, No.94, 1965), Current Tissue Literature by M.R. Murray and G. Kopech. New York, October House (1965), V: 29 (1965)

5. Thomas, F.L.: And Cramer, L.M.: *A Chamber and Perfusion system or Generalized and Specialized in Vitro*

Studies. Texas Reports Biol. Med., 24:700-11 (1966)

6. Thomas, F.L.: And Cramer, L.M.: *Biaxial, Oriented Polystyrene: An inert Substrate and Diffusion Membrane for use in Tissue Culture.* Texas Reports Biol. Med. 24:712-19 (1966).

7. Thomas, F.L.: *The Role of History in Black Power.* Black Power Conference, Newark, N.J. (1967)

8. Thomas, F.L.: *A New Perfusion System for General and Specific in Vitro Continuous Growth Cultures.* In Vitro, Ann. Symposium Abstract, Tissue Culture Assoc. Vol. 111 p.173 (1968)

9. Thomas, F.L.: Sherman F. Stewart, J.W. Parker, J Putterman, J. G. and Margoliash, E.: *The Mutational Alteration of Iso-l-cytochrome (c) from Yeast.*

10. (Gordisky, R. Tanner, T. and Thomas, F.: technical assistance), United States Atomic Energy Commission at the University of Rochester Atomic Energy Project, Rochester, New York. Report No. UR-49-918.

11. Gilmore, R.A., Stewart, J.W. and Sherman, F.: *Amino acid replacements resulting from super- suppression of a nonsense mutant of yeast, technical assistance*: Shipman, N., Thomas, F.L. and Regan, P.) Biochim, Biophysic Acta, 161, pp. 270-272 (1968)

12. Sherman F., Stewart, J.W., Parker, J., Inhaber, E. and Shipman, N.A.: *The Mutational Alteration of the Primary Structure of Yeast Iso-l cytochrome c* (technical assistance: Campbell, W., Thomas, F.L. and McLaughlin, E.P.). Jour. Biol. Chem. 243:20, pp., 5446-5456, October 25, (1968)

13. Sherman, F., Stewart, J.W., Cravens, M., Thomas, F.L. and Shipman, N.: *different action of UV on a nonsense codon located at two different positions in the iso-lcytochrome c gene of yeast,* Genetics 61, s55 (1969).

14. Stewart, J.W., Sherman, F., Shipman, N, Thomas, F.L., and Cravens, M.: *Longer and Shorter Chain Initiator Mutants of Baker's Yeast, Federation* Proc. 28, 597 (1969)

15. Thomas, F.L.: And Cramer, L.M.: Thomas and Cramer chamber in *Methods in Microbiology* edited by J.R. Norris and D.W. Ribbons. Academic Press, London and New York. Vol. I, Chapter X Section (j), pp. 395, 404, 424, (1969)

16. Lawrence, C.W., Stewart, J.W., Sherman, F. and Thomas, F.L.: *Mutagenesis in Ultraviolet-sensitive mutants of yeast.* (Genetics 64:S36-S37 (1970)

17. Poyton, R.O. and Branton, D.: *A Multipurpose Micro perfusion Chamber Experimental Cell Research* 60, 109-114 (1970). Cited on p.113, 114: F.L. Thomas and L.M.

Cramer.

18. Gilmore, R.A., Stewart, J.W., and Sherman, F.: *Amino Acid Replacement resulting from super- suppression of nonsense mutants of iso- cytochrome c from yeast.* (Thomas, F.L., Shipman and Regan, P., technical assistance). J. Mol Biol. 61

19. Stewart, J.W. Sherman, F., Shipman, N.A. and Jackson, M.: *Identification and Mutational Relocation of the AUG Codon Initiating Translation of Iso-l-cytochrome c in Yeast.* (Thomas, F.L., Brockman, N. and Risen, E., technical assistance) J. Biol. Chem. 246:24, 7429-7445 (1971)

20. Thomas, F.L.: *Perfusion Staining and Microphotography of Viable Cells in The Thomas- Cramer Perfusion Chamber.* (Paper read before the 4th International Congress of Cytology; London, England, (May 1971)

Invited participation in the following:

∞ West African Historical Society Conference- Sierra Leone (April 1971);

∞ 3rd International Congress of Experimental Cytology Rio Janeiro, Brazil (May 1968);

∞ Annual Conference on Photography for Scientists

and Engineers Boston (June 1968);

∞ Tissue Culture Association-Puerto Rico (June1968);

∞ 12th International Congress of the History of Science-Paris, France (August 1968);

∞ 21st International Congress of the History of Medicine-Siena, Italy (September1968);

∞ 2nd International Congress of the Transplantation Society, New York (Fall, 1968);

∞ 7th International Congress International Academy of Pathology-Milan, Italy (September 5-11, 1968);

∞ XI International Congress of Microbiological Standardization-Milan, Italy (September 16-20, 1968);

∞ The American Electroencephalographic Society Meeting-San Francisco, Calif. (September 12-15, 1968);

∞ XII International Congress of Cell Biology, Brussels, Belgium (August 25-31, 1968);

∞ 3rd International Health Conference, Copenhagen, Denmark (August, 1968);

∞ 12th International Congress of Genetics, Tokyo (August 1968);

∞ 11th Congreso de la Asociacion Latinoamericana de Sociedades de Biologia

∞ Medicina Nuclear-Buenos Aires, (November 14-17, 1968);

∞ 10thAll-Pakistan Medical Conference, Dacca (November 14-17, 1968);

Memberships and Honors:

Member of the Royal of Health (London), 1969

Member of the Royal Canadian Institute, (Toronto), 1969

Invited Membership:

Association Internationale D' Orientation Scolaire ET Professionelle, (Luxembourg), 1969

Invited participation:

Third International Symposium on Yeasts, (The Hague), June 2-6th, 1969

17th Annual Meeting Radiation Research Society Cincinnati, May 18-22, 1969

Second International Conference on Medical Physics (Boston), August 11-15, 1969

Guest Lecturer:

Black Youth Organization, (Newark, N.J.) 1969

Combined Faculties of The Rochester Colgate Divinity School
and St. Bernard's Seminary, (Rochester), 1969

Association International Des Sciences De l' Education, (Paris,
France), 1969

Black Student Organization, Oberlin College (Oberlin, Ohio),
1969

Invited participant:

Jack and Jill Inc, Rochester Chapter, Rochester, N.Y. 1969;

15th International Convention on Civilization Diseases, Vital
Substances, Nutrition, (Hanover, West Germany), (1969)

Third Congress of The Organ Transplantation Society, (Rome
Italy), (1969)

54th Meeting of the Association for the Study of Negro Life &
History (Birmingham, Alabama) (1969)

Fourth Annual Illinois Conference on Afro American History,
Northern Illinois, University of DeKalb, Illinois, (1969)
Annual Alumni Award for 1969,Wagner College, Staten Island,
New York), (1969)

Invitations, Honors and Participations:

Black Student Union, Monroe Community College, Rochester,
NY, (lecture) (1970)

Exhibition from private collection: 40 posters in the Rochester,
NY Midtown Plaza for Rochester Chapter of the National

Association of Negro Business and Professional Women's Club Inc., Rochester, NY (1970)

Annual Meeting of the International Platform Association, Washington D.C. (1970)

First International Congress of Immunology, Washington, D.C. (1970)

Intercontinental Biographical Association, Dartmouth, England (1970)

The Institute for Advanced Technology, Washington, D.C. (1970)

1970 (Tentative)

Panelist: Monroe Community College, Rochester, N.Y. (1970); Third Annual Conference: Association of Afro American Educators, Washington D.C. (1970)

The 13th Annual Meeting of the Society for the History of Technology, Chicago, Illinois (1970)

72nd General Meeting, Archaeological Institute of America, New York City (1970)

The Western Society of Naturalists, Honolulu, Hawaii (1970)

History of Science Society, Chicago, Illinois (1970)

Intercontinental Biographical Association Dartmouth: Devon England (1970)

Creative and Successful Personalities of the World, Los Angeles, Calif. (1970)

Symposium on Microwave Power, Monterey Calif. (1971);

Participant (paper presented) Fourth International Congress of Cytology, London, England (1971)

Black History Exhibit for National Association of Negro Business and Professional Clubs, Inc., Rochester, NY (1971)

Invited Exhibitor:

Rochester Museum and Science Center, Rochester, NY 1971

Lecture:

Black Student Association: St. John Fisher College Rochester, NY (1971)

Invited Participation:

72nd Meeting, American Society of Microbiology, Philadelphia, Pa. (1972)

University of Rochester Personnel Department:

In a letter dated October 7, 1976, Priscilla G. Specht, Personnel Representative of Technical Positions at the University of Rochester stated, "Mr. Thomas joined the staff of the University of Rochester Medical Center on January 9, 1961, and was a highly valued and widely respected member of the University family until his untimely death on February 24, 1974. She further stated that,

As a Technical Associate in Radiation Biology and Biophysics, he made important contributions to the scientific work of the Medical Center. One of his major achievements during his years of service here was the development of a Chamber and Perfusion System for General and Specialized In Vitro Studies. He described this project in these terms:

In order to stimulate the cellular environment, in vitro perfusion techniques must fulfill many requirements. The following constitute the major criteria, which must be met:

1. Regulated supply flowing nutrient,

2. Controlled temperatures,

3. Provision for removal and collection of spent medium and metabolic by-products,

4. Sterility,

5. Inertness of all parts,

6. Accessibility to tissues, cells and media for analyses and modifications,

7. Option of longer or short term cultures,

8. Chamber portability for varied microscopy and photomicrography,

9. Design simplicity that favors handling ease, smooth performance and low cost.

"The system fully met all of these objectives, and the achievement was characteristic of the man," Specht said. "He was a gentleman and scholar."

"I'm just a natural man, one of the common folks who enjoy reading and studying and helping people. I like plain clothes, plain food and good friends"-Dr. Freddie Thomas

The funeral was officiated by Reverend Marvin Chandler on Sunday, March 3, in 1974 at 3:00 PM, in the Interfaith Chapel of the University of Rochester, Riverside Campus.

Freddie's obituary summed up the life he lived in a few words as, *sincere, earnest, loyal, industrious and self-sacrificing.*

John Griffin, a close friend of the Thomases' called him a gadfly, who created a synergistic atmosphere that brought youngsters clamoring for knowledge at all hours.

"Freddie always had time 'not' only for youngsters, but anyone who wanted to check-out the authenticity of his work," Griffin added. "Freddie was the type of individual who could stand toe-to-toe with the best of the professional and scientific technologists in the United States and the world."

"Freddie's extensive study and research in tissue culture and the fact, he was able to physically translate his idea into an invention which aided and supported his theories are indications of his extraordinary intellect, talent and creative power," he said. "I'm not a doctor, but I believe, when you're full of anxiety and exuberance and is not able to have the time or convenience and most important the source to relate to, that's not good for anyone's body; especially a fellow with multiple myeloma. We know of no other one who tried harder to interpret the wishes of men. He may have been small in stature but Freddie's love and devotion for his wife, his concern for others. And the character and integrity he possessed made him ten feet tall," Griffin said. He led and served, he is just away."

The attendees were transfixed in a perpetual solemn as the ushers slowly escorted his casket to the awaiting hearse. People were hesitant to leave. They weren't ready to deal with Freddie being gone.

Back home on Skuse Street, Midge was never alone for nearly a year. People came early in the morning and some came late at night, who were concerned about keeping her from grieving.

The unwavering support from the community intensified a passion within Midge to continue Freddie's work. She began by establishing the Freddie Thomas Scholarship Fund for high school seniors majoring in S.T.E.M. fields.

"I wanted to continue what Freddie started and many of his students and friends wanted to honor his legacy in similar ways," Midge said. "A gentleman out of Boston, Massachusetts by the name of Octavius Rowe requested my permission to name his school's library Dr. Freddie Thomas Memorial Library, in his honor."

The Roxbury Medical Technical Institute, where the library will be housed provides educational opportunities and facilities for disadvantaged students from the Roxbury-Dorchester, Massachusetts's area. The school commitment includes increasing the quality and amount of health care in the area.

Freddie met Rowe when he was invited to address The Second International Conference on Medical Physics in Boston, Massachusetts in 1969.

Rowe, a graduate student at the time questioned Freddie's research repeatedly during the lecture. When the session ended, Freddie allowed Rowe to read information from several books published by well-respected persons of the academia field, where the research was drawn from. Then Freddie asked Rowe for his proof, which he was unable to produce. That encounter led to a long-standing stewardship between the two.

"The function of the institute is to encourage community participation in social services," Rowe said. "Because it attracts black people back into the community. The school is self-help personified. At present, only four black doctors are practicing in Roxbury and Dorchester."

"Because they do not have the proper role models, many of the students don't see possibilities," Rowe added. "The Institute's program enables 8 to 18-year old students to work with educators, students, and pre medical students at Boston hospitals and educational institutions to motivate them to enter the medical profession."

After Freddie's death, Midge received dozens of request from people and institutions seeking to honor his legacy. So she decided, if people were memorializing him outside of Rochester, then something honoring Freddie, should be establish where his legacy was born.

The Internal Revenue Service approved Midge's request to convene, The Freddie Thomas Foundation on July 9, 1974, as a not-for-profit charitable corporation.

The acting officials of the Foundation's Board of Directors included: John Griffin as president; Midge Thomas as founder; Eugene Parrs as secretary.

While in search for the ideal building to house the

foundation, Griffin recalls a conversation he was having with Freddie as they passed the Harro East Building at 380 Andrews Street.

"Freddie directed me to stop the car on the corner of Liberty Pole Way and Andrews Street," Griffin said. "And strangely enough, I remember him pointing at the Harro East Building and saying, if it's God's aspiration, one day he would be able to buy a building like that and give it to the community."

Since 1931, the seven stories, 26,000 sq. ft. site has housed the Jewish Young Men and Women Hebrew Association.

The building consisted of an auditorium, swimming pool, gymnasium, handball courts, kitchen, and restaurant, dormitories and meeting rooms.

The Jewish Community Center of Greater Rochester owned the property. The property went up for sale, when the current Jewish center was built in Brighton in 1973.

Obtaining the building was a unique opportunity for a relatively new foundation to be able to own a multipurpose property that has value and convenience that was incomparable in the building market then.

Griffin's resources as Realtor and Freddie's interaction with the Jewish community, where he was affectionately known as the Little Rabbi allowed a quick purchase and transfer.

Freddie's vision to occupy the Harro East Building became a tangible reality on September 27, 1974. The building was renamed, *Triangle Community Center.*

"The new name was based on the fact that the building is shaped like a triangle and the objectives of the center are triangular, such as: environmental, sociological and physical," Griffin said.

An undertaking of such magnitude was unheard of for any community oriented black group in the Rochester area. The foundation transformed the building into an excellent resource facility for resident programs.

Over 200 community service organizations and several job-training programs used the center for their training site.

Some other entities included hospitals, veteran agencies, settlement houses, local churches as well as individuals.

The Olympic size swimming pool was the home for the city of Rochester Natatorium. And was equipped with several other recreational entities that enabled its flexibility to accommodate various activities at any given time that included basketball teams from Xerox, Kodak, Rochester Products, and Bausch & Lomb.

The 1000 seat auditorium theatre conducted entertainment concerts featuring, the Rochester Philharmonic Orchestra, Al Jerreau, Don Potter, Aunt Ester, Lilac Queen Pageant, Black Friars, B.B. King, Millie Jackson, and the Nigerian Independence Reception.

The adjacent Kitchen accommodated social events for family and school reunions, wedding receptions, dances, parties, movies, exhibits and graduations.

On Columbus Day in 1976, The Freddie Thomas Foundation and the Jewish Community Center of Greater Rochester held a joint ceremony for the removal of the building's cornerstone that was instituted in 1931 and replaced with the laying of the new cornerstone of the Triangle Community Center.

A 'time capsule' filled with letters from more than 100 organizations and individuals were also placed behind the new cornerstone.

John Griffin, president of The Freddie Thomas Foundation and Sanford Liebschutz, president of the Jewish Community Center, Board of Directors presided over the ceremony.

A statement from the Jewish Community Center read:

"For over 40 years, the Jewish Community Center was the home of the Jewish Young Men and Women's Association. It was a central meeting place of the Jewish Community and served their recreational and cultural needs for those many years and for two decades previously in other close-by locations. As the center of Jewish population moved away from the urban core, we moved to new facilities, leaving behind this large building. When we learned of the interest of the Freddie Thomas Foundation in acquiring the building to operate a new community center, we were most happy that we could arrange for you to acquire it. It gives us great satisfaction to know that again our former home is dedicated to serving the cultural and recreational needs of the residents of the urban center, helping them to deal with the realities and concerns of everyday life, as it did for members of the Jewish Community for many years. "

Rochester Mayor Thomas J. Ryan made brief remarks before introducing Midge to an audience of more than 300 people.

"It belongs to the community," Midge said. "And the more the community supports it, the faster it will grow. Freddie envisioned a community center composed of the community, whose purpose was to provide services for the community. We're talking about producing benefits to the community rather than just consuming, with no return."

Midge Thomas removing the 1931 cornerstone of the Jewish Young
Men and Women Hebrew Association (1976)

Former Republican congressional member (1963-1993) and Rochester
City Councilman (1955-1961) Frank Horton sings at the Triangle
Community Center. (June 1977)

Former Mayor William Bill Johnson (1994-2005) opens Triangle

Community Center 'time capsule' on the center's 30th Anniversary

(May 1974-2004)

"A lie needs many props to try to hold it up. The truth needs no prop. It can stand on its own"-Dr. Freddie Thomas

"Brother Freddie's dedication to connecting our history to a rich and beautiful heritage through documented research enables us to embrace his spiritual presence and to share his knowledge again," said journalist Adolf Dupree. "He is alive and well in room 205 on the 2nd floor of the Triangle Community Center. He is alive in his collection of books and papers and personal possessions set up as a display of black pride in all its glory. He invites you to examine his invention of creating an atmosphere outside of the body to grow and examine cells and to listen to his last, but timely words of wisdom on the necessity of education and self-sufficiency," Dupree said. "Many people who were influenced by Freddie took on the task to honor him, as if it was their responsibility to keep his legacy alive.

On Saturday nights, the center's theatre was filled with hundreds of people there to see; The Thomas Players perform *"Up the Street,"* a play based on the life of Freddie.

The Thomas Players, a multicultural theater group is organized to present events that dramatize the achievements and contributions of significant citizens in the community.

Scenes reenacted from Freddie's life featured memorable instances that brought the spiritual essence of his philosophy back to the forefront.

The Black History Month celebration concluded with a reading of a proclamation from the city of Rochester that honored the lifelong works of Freddie and hometown abolitionist Frederick Douglass.

The proclamation stated that:

"Afro-American History Month provides an opportunity for all of us to increase our awareness of the contributions Black Americans have made to our nation and to our community, and it is with special pride that we take this occasion to salute two particularly prominent Black Americans whose names and accomplishments will forever be in the minds and hearts of all Rochesterians and Frederick Douglass, one of Rochester's greatest Black citizens, exhibited unparalleled initiative and intelligence in his role as writer, orator, statesman, diplomat and international leader in the struggle for freedom, and he brought great pride to the city of Rochester through his publication of 'The North Star,' while leading the fight

against slavery."

"And Freddie L. Thomas, another of the most notable Black citizens of Rochester, was an internationally acclaimed historian of Black Culture; his expertise included not only the Rochester community, but the nation and Africa as well, and as a University of Rochester biologist, his scientific reputation is well-respected among scholars; his versatility embraced song-writing and science, and he has been cited in several different 'Who's Who In America,' volumes, and today the Triangle Community Center and its library, both established in his memory by the Freddie Thomas Foundation, are a monument to the man and his life."

Speaking on Freddie's behalf Midge said, it's essential that older people mentor young folks in their communities to close the gap between the generations, which she believes is one of the problems leaving adults and the youth population unable to make a purposeful connection.

She challenged the kids to go home and ask their grandparents about some of the stories their grandparents told them.

"In doing so, they will have some personal stories to understand," Midge explained. "There were some people that came up from the South and went through a struggle these kids know nothing about. They see it on television, but for the majority of this generation, they don't know their great grandmother or great grandfather may have been involved. When I'm watching documentaries and see those people at night time using the Underground Railroad going through farmland and traveling all night long with no sleep," she asked. Do we stop and think about how they ate? How they went to use the bathroom? How they changed their clothes and didn't take a bath?" she said. "Now think about the daily things we go through and here they had to go from North Carolina to Canada on foot. Could you do it? She implied. "That's dedication! That's saying I want to get out of that oppressive lifestyle. And I am not going to take it any more. When our children see the struggle on television, they can't make the connection, but the people they're looking at expressing incredible ingenuity in the face of injustice are their blood ancestors."

Freddie was being recognized for the second time by the city of Rochester in 1984.

He was included in '*The 84 Rochesterians Sesquicentennial, 4 Score & 4.*'

As an inductee, Freddie is highlighted as one of eighty-four persons who made significant contributions to Rochester.

The ceremony included a parade through downtown. Dr. Anthony L. Jordan and Frederick Douglass are the only other persons of color to make the list of eighty-four.

My Friend Margaret "Midge" Thomas

Many years have passed since I met Midge Thomas. It was 1957. I was 13 years old. Our initial meeting was approximately 57 years ago. My how time flies.

The day I saw the Thomases for the first time it was beyond my comprehension that initial meeting would anchor a lifelong friendship. On a little street, on the eastside of the city, I remember the day they moved into their home that sat directly across the street from us.

It seemed as though the movers would never stop bringing things into their house. I remember thinking what kind of neighbors would they be? Would they like children? Do they have a dog or a cat? Were they mean or friendly?

It was a few years before our families connected as friends. My little sister Arneska at 8 years old had quite a singing voice. Midge was the president, founder and a charter member of the Rochester Genesee Valley Club of the National Association of Negro Business and Professional Women's Clubs. The club's national convention was coming up in Boston, Massachusetts and they were in need of a singer.

Midge heard Arneska sing in church and if you know

anything about Midge, she's not afraid to approach and ask a favor. She meets no strangers and quietly gets things done. My sister's performance at the club's national convention was the beginning of a lifelong family friendship.

Midge was also the owner and personal designer of *Original Creations*. Wedding accessories and fashion show productions were her signatures. It was not uncommon to see-ladies coming in and out of her home wearing fancy hats and gloves that accentuated designs of upscale fashion.

Midge flanked by Original Creations Fashion models

Midge was a bubbling socialite who enjoyed hosting club and committee meetings and hat and tea parties. One of the most memorable times for me was the first time I saw a native African getting out of an automobile and going into the Thomases' home.

This opened my imagination to a whole new world. The Thomases' hosted receptions for African ambassadors, prime ministers, and monarchs. The distinguished guests would be adorned in an array of colors and all types of beautiful headdresses. It was my first real cultural and emotional attachment to Africa, so watching them arrive was magnificent. I never forgot it, and I hold it dear to my heart. I knew one day I would travel to Africa, which I did to Ghana many years later in 2012.

As the years passed, Midge and my mother Mrs. Ruby Harvey became friends as well as good neighbors. They started *Skuse Street Neighborhood Block Club* and was instrumental in establishing, *Coalition of Northeast Association (Conea)*.

The organization serves the community in the northeast area of the city and continues to thrive today.

The friendship between our families has also lasted until

this day and continues to grow through my sister Arneska, my husband Cleveland and myself, despite the lost of Dr. Thomas and my mother and father.

Midge is a visionary leader embodied with concerns regarding social injustice in our communities. She's one of the first African American women to sit on many boards and committees in the city of Rochester to promote societal change. Midge's community service and volunteering spans over 60 plus years.

Margaret 'Midge' Thomas is my friend and mentor. Her gifts, talents and organizational skills are many. Dr. Thomas was a great man indeed in his own right, but a great woman stood beside him in her own right.

Respectfully,

Martha L. Scofield-Hope, President of Rochester

Genesee Valley Club of The National Association of Negro

Business and Professional Women's Club Inc.,

"I believe the volunteer part of public service is who we are as human beings"-Midge Thomas

Midge became known for her natural tendency to volunteer for duties concerning public service.

She was awarded, the National Sojourner Truth Award, the city of Rochester Black Heritage Award, the National Achievement Award, and the National Jefferson Award for Public Service, just to name a few.

As a life member of AME Zion Church and as a charter member of Rochester Genesee Valley Club, Midge continues to highlight the importance of awarding scholarships to deserving seniors headed to college. The club, now in its 57th year has preserved its mission to:

"Seek out women in the community that are culturally sensitive and aware, dedicated to the purpose of working for the community, in the community, and to resolve to do all they can to leave the community better than they found it."

The club's mission statement is illustrated in her aspiration to establish a public drinking fountain downtown.

After picking up some medication from a pharmacy to combat her flu symptoms, Midge was unable to make it

173

home, so she entered a downtown restaurant and requested a cup of water to drink along with the pill.

The waiter requested she pay 10 cents for a Styrofoam cup, which she believed was an overreached because her perspective is that water is free. The incident disturbed her, as did a report in which a senior citizen of the community was in need of water for medical purposes while downtown and none was accessible. The encounter with the waiter made her empathetic to others who at any moment could be in a similar situation and she felt it was unfair.

The '*We Care Committee,*' of the Freddie Thomas Foundation convened on the issue after Midge submitted a proposal to donate a public drinking fountain to the city.

In 1986, the board approved the project. The undertaking involved more than 80 community members of all races and creeds working together.

Rochester Downtown Development Corporation facilitated a worldwide search for the ideal fountain before settling on a 3-faucet fountain made of bronze that was inspired by a Japanese Architect.

In July 1988, the committee came up with the name, '*Miss Jane Pittman Public Drinking Fountain.*'

The novel, '*The Autobiography of Miss Jane Pittman,*'

written by Ernest Gaines, inspired the name.

The fountain honors a fictional black woman (portrayed in the movie by Cicely Tyson) who showed great courage and determination when she finally drank from a water fountain that for years was available to 'whites only'.

"Miss Pittman overcame the oppression of segregation by drinking from the fountain that gave victory to the ideals of equality, liberty, and humanity," Midge said.

Although the character of Miss Jane Pittman is fictional some say, she stands as a strong symbol of courage and freedom.

The Brighton-Pittsford Post reported that, "Many who have read Gaines novel which was later adapted into a famed television movie in 1974, are surprised to learn, Pittman was not a real person. Even so, the movie served as a crucial breakthrough for future television dramas such as Roots. Funding for the project has involved private funding and a variety of activities, including small donations, even pennies, by young school children, giving them the opportunity to feel a part of the Miss Jane Pittman Drinking Fountain belonged to them," the newspaper reported.

"The largest fund-raising event was the Lilac Festival Gala

and An Evening of Elegance, which Gaines attended as the guest of honor. Gaines cited honors the book had received since its publication in 1971, but not until recently did anyone ever think about dedicating a water fountain to a character in a book."

"My publisher thought the request was a hoax, and for a while, I did too," Gaines said. "But Midge kept calling me and asking if she could use the name from the book, and then asked if I could come for fundraising and for this dedication. I said no at first, that I was a busy man, but she is just as determined as the character in the book, and here I am."

A replica of the fountain created by Calvin Hubbard, an art teacher at East High School and owner of Turtle Pottery Gallery was unveiled at the gala. Mayor Ryan and County Executive Thomas Frey delivered a joint proclamation and encouraged all residents to drink from the water fountain and remember the principles represented in the character of Miss Jane Pittman.

"As of today, May 19, 1989, the city of Rochester has proclaimed to represent, *Miss Jane Pittman Day*," the mayor said. "It was most fitting, the drinking fountain be placed downtown at Liberty Pole Plaza. The site of many flagpoles has long symbolized freedom."

The fountain was installed July 30, 1989. A plaque designed by Midge's sister Helen Corley was added to the fountain in the fall and the Rochester City School District developed a black history curriculum using Gaines book, as a method for teaching students about the Civil Rights Movement. The city held a ceremony to celebrate the 25th Anniversary of the Miss Jane Pittman Public Drinking Fountain, on July 30, 2014.

Rochester's first female Mayor Lovely A. Warren, proclaimed the day, Margaret 'Midge' Thomas Day.

"The three faucet fountain represents more than just a drink of water," Midge explained. "The faucets represent liberty, equality and humanity. Water is the most significant part of life, running abundantly and freely through the greater part of Earth and human bodies. In its flow it represents activity and progress. In its clarity, it represents good foresight and in its purity, it represents good will."

Midge Thomas, Mayor Thomas Ryan (1974-1994), and Writer Ernest
Gaines (Autobiography of Miss Jane Pittman) holding hands over the
fountain. (July 30,1989)

Educator and Rochester Community Activist Iris Banister speak to a crowd of more than 7,000 during the fountain's inauguration ceremony.

(Seated from left to right-Midge, Mayor Ryan and Ernest Gaines)

Rochester Mayor Thomas Ryan and Midge enjoying the ceremonial
dedication of Miss Jane Pittman Public Drinking Fountain (July 30,
1989)

Rochester Mayor Robert Duffy (2006-2010) rededication of the
fountain's plaque (May 2008)

Presentation of a check for $5,000 to the city of Rochester by Midge
Thomas for Miss Jane Pittman Public Drinking Fountain

"Don't foster negative thoughts. Always think positive and choose your battles. Every situation doesn't deserve your attention"-Midge Thomas

After twenty years, The Freddie Thomas Foundation needed to reorganize and realign its focus. The first phase was to develop Triangle Square Center, at 1180 East Main Street in 1994.

The new center was intended to be one of Rochester's main resource facilities to provide social, educational and cultural special events at low overhead cost to supplant the mission of the larger Triangle Community Center.

Journalist Shirley Thompson, of the Frederick Douglass Voice, reported that Walter Robinson, creator of the Rochester Calendar of Black Events was the first to use the 26,000 sq. ft. facility.

Discussing with a reporter, the need for black people to keep more dollars in the community, Robinson says, we aren't even close. "The money from 95 percent of black paid events does not go to black party houses."

Midge agreed with Robinson but suggested to the reporter, the opportunity now exists.

"Triangle Square Center is a party house and much more, plus it belongs to the community," she added. "The Freddie Thomas Foundation will provide the space as a public service. It will charge only enough rent to cover expenses and subsidize the cost to organizations that can't pay." Midge has served throughout her tenure as a non-paid employee for both centers and The Freddie Thomas Foundation. Her responsibilities included supervision of the center and building maintenance, organizing work experience training programs, coordinating and supervising special projects, and manager of emergency and permanent residents in the center and liaison representative for Triangle Square's tenants and the administration office.

She averaged a work schedule of more than 12 hours per day, 7 days per week.

In 1977, Midge signed an 'Affirmation of Voluntary Service,' for any duties, she performed working at the centers and the foundation. The Freddie Thomas Foundation honored Midge in 1994, for two decades of volunteer and community service at a tributary event.

Midge Thomas working the phones at the Triangle

Community Center (May 1976)

City of Rochester presents Midge with a proclamation honoring over a
'50 years' of public service

CURRICULUM VITAE

Margaret Thomas

Born: September 10, 1926,

                 Rochester, NY

Married: Freddie Thomas, February 9, 1957

Parents: Milton and Ethel Banks

Siblings: Brothers: Charles and George

                 Sister: Helen Corley

Education:

-Caledonia High School, Rochester, New York

-Adrianne School of Beauty Culture

-Rochester Business Institute

-Rochester Institute of Technology (Tailoring)

-Academy of Millinery Design, Orange, NJ

-Gabriel Richard Self Development

Experience:

-Orchid Beauty Salon, Owner & Manager (1954)

-Original Creations Bridal Accessories, Owner & Manager (1958)

-Rochester Genesee Valley Club, National Assoc. Negro Business & Professional Women's Club, Inc., co founder & President (1958)

Experience:

-Dr. Freddie Thomas Scholarship Fund, Founder (1974-2007)

-Freddie Thomas Foundation, Founder (1974-2009)

-Triangle Community Center, Executive Director (1974-1982)

-Triangle Square Center, Executive Director (1994-1998)

-Miss Jane Pittman Drinking Fountain, Founder (1989)

-Liberty Pole Block Club, Founder (2001)

-Dr. Freddie Thomas High School

-Ambassadors Program, Founder (2007)

-Officer Al Smith Memorial Garden at Dr. Freddie

-Thomas High School, Founder (2002)

-DELEA Dance Lovers, cofounder (2008)

Board of Directors:

-Rochester Chapter American Red Cross

-Salvation Army Women's Auxiliary

-Rochester Genesee Valley Club, National Assoc. Negro Business and Professional Women's Club, Inc. (President 1958)

-Women's Coalition for Downtown

-Zonta Club of Rochester, President (1980)

-Ralph Bunch Scholarship Fund

-The Freddie Thomas Foundation

-Honorary, Rose & Joseph Denaro

-Interfaith Center Contact of Rochester

Memberships:

-Alpha Psi Omega Sorority & Fraternity

-Troubadours Choir

-Alzheimer Minority Outreach Advisory

-City Vision 2000 Committee

-Rochester Events Network

-Toastmasters International

-New York State Federated Women's Club

-Rochester Citizens Police Academy

National Awards & Recognitions:

-Honorable Mention Gannett Times Union, Club Women of the Year Award (1969)

-Roch. Negro Bus. & Prof., Women's Club, Business Award (1975)

-American Institute of Public Affairs, Jefferson Award (1982)

-Nat. Assoc., Negro Bus. & Prof, Women's National Achievement Award (1982)

-NYS Division for Youth Foster Parent, Certificate of Appreciation (1982)

-Roch. Downtown Program Trust Fund, Rochester Volunteerism Award (1990)

-Main Event '90, Rochester Voluntarism Award (1990)

-Roch. Gen., Valley Club NANBPW Inc., National Sojourner Truth Award (1991)

-Zonta Club of Rochester, Heart Award (1991)

-Chamber of Commerce, Women in Business Award (1991)

-Rochester Women Chamber of Commerce, Nominee

-ATHENA Award (1994)

-First Church Divine Duke Ellington, Hall of Fame
Award (1994)

-Freddie Thomas Foundation, Salute to Midge Thomas
(1994)

-Rochester City School Board of Education, Salute to
Midge Thomas (1998)

Local Awards & Recognitions:

-Lena Gantt, Distinguished Community Service Award

-United Way, J.C. Penney Golden Rule Award

-Rochester Above, Community Service Award

-City of Rochester Black Heritage Committee, Pioneer
Award

-Theta Omicron Chapter, Omega Psi Phi Fraternity,

-Outstanding Community Service Award

-City of Rochester, Story Art Award

-Memorial AME Zion Church, Church Mother's Club

-Asante Sana Award, Community Service

-Metropolitan Women's Network, Empowerment
Women's Award

-Action for Better Community, Community Service Award

-Paradise Temple #1149, Love Never Gives Up Award

-Freddie Thomas Foundation, Volunteer of the Year

Sankofa Organization, Outstanding Community Leaders

"Just because someone is certified does not necessarily mean that they are qualified"-Dr. Freddie Thomas

One of Freddie's most memorable quotes is, "I know without a doubt that I can build the finest school this community has ever seen, I will not do it. When the people are ready, they will build it themselves and then they will come and place me in my rightful position."

In 1994, Freddie's prophetic quote manifested when the community chose to name a newly built school at 625 Scio Street in his honor, *Dr. Freddie Thomas Learning Center.*

Midge said Freddie was not the sort of man who would have expected such honors for his efforts. Yet, he was certainly a man worth honoring.

"His efforts in teaching were not for anything else except for, to raise the standards," she said. "I think that was his lifelong dream."

The name of the school was chosen from over 100 entries submitted by area residents. The Northeast Middle School Planning Committee, a coalition of residents, community agencies and school district staff organized the contest.

The contest was open to anyone who lived in the northeast

part of the city. The committee members were looking for someone who could set an example of high achievement to name the building after, preferably, but not limited to, a local person.

This would be someone who could be a role model to area students, especially those who will be attending the new school. Once all the names were submitted, a subcommittee made up of planning committee members, parents and city school district staff; selected the winning entry. The final choice would then have to be approved by the school board. Members of the board were unanimous in naming the school in honor of Freddie.

Board Member Frank Willis, who grew up a few blocks from Freddie, made the motion. Board Member Daryl Porter seconded it.

"You didn't just learn math, science or English from him; you learned how to be a better person," Commissioner Willis said. "He taught me as a boy that it was possible to be cool and smart."

The Dr. Freddie Thomas Learning Center became a new idea of community schools. This was part to the residents' involvement in the planning of the school and its relationship to the community.

The committee had a voice into several aspects of the school's development. They discussed what services would go into the human services wing that will house a branch of the Lewis Street Center, the selection of the school principal, the hiring of teachers, and the method teachers will use in the classroom.

Rochester City School District
Board of Education
Resolution No. 94-95: 790 (6)

By Member of the Board Frank Willis -

Whereas, the Board of Education has adopted the policy of naming our schools, wherever practicable, after some worthy and well-known person; and

Whereas, the late Dr. Freddie Thomas, born February 10, 1918, was a respected scientist, educator, and humanitarian who did extensive research in genetics and plastic surgery at the University of Rochester; and

Whereas, in his lifelong dedication to learning, Dr. Freddie Thomas tutored and encouraged high school and college "drop-outs" to resume their education, and opened his home as a center of learning, discussion, and inspiration for friends from around the world; and

Whereas, the legacy of Dr. Freddie Thomas as a black scholar, scientist, inventor, and humanitarian is one to be preserved and emulated; and

Whereas, the new middle school in Rochester's northeast area will be opening in September 1995, dedicated to excellence in education and service to the community; and

Whereas, with the support of the Lewis Street Center and other community agencies, this school will serve as a neighborhood resource dedicated to meeting the social, health, economic and educational needs of all people who want to learn; and

Whereas, members of the community surrounding the school have been involved in all aspects of its development, from curriculum design to building layout, making it a true community school; and

Whereas, this strong community involvement has included a recommendation to name the school in honor of Dr. Freddie Thomas; therefore be it

Resolved, That, the new northeast middle school be, and it hereby is, named,

"Dr. Freddie Thomas Learning Center"

Seconded by Member of the Board Darryl Porter.

Adopted unanimously.

Archie C. Curry
President

Loretta D. Johnson
Interim Superintendent of Schools

May 4, 1995

COMMITTEE ON THE BUDGET

COMMITTEE ON GOVERNMENT
REFORM AND OVERSIGHT

CONGRESSIONAL ARTS CAUCUS

CAUCUS FOR WOMEN'S ISSUES

NEW AGRICULTURE CAUCUS

AT LARGE

2347 RAYBURN HOUSE OFFICE BUILDING
WASHINGTON, D.C. 20515
202/225 3615

DISTRICT OFFICE
3120 FEDERAL BUILDING
100 STATE STREET
ROCHESTER, NY 14614
716/232 4850
TTY 716 454 4655

CONGRESS OF THE UNITED STATES

LOUISE M. SLAUGHTER
28TH DISTRICT, NEW YORK

May 4, 1995

Ms. Midge Thomas
President
The Freddie Thomas Foundation
1160 East Main St.
Rochester, New York 14609

Dear Ms. Thomas:

It has come to my attention that the Rochester City School
District has decided to name the new northeast middle school "The
Freddie Thomas Learning Center". I am thrilled that the school
district chose to name the school in honor of your husband. Dr.
Thomas gave so much of himself to the Rochester community. It is
only appropriate that his memory is preserved through the
institution of education.

Congratulations for this wonderful recognition!

Sincerely,

Louise Slaughter
Member of Congress

LMS/js

197

The Marketview Heights newsletter reported that, committee members wanted to see priority for enrollment go to neighborhood children. Although the city school district has an open enrollment policy, preference would be given to those who live in the surrounding area. This is a part of a move to bring back the idea of students going to school near where they live, in which the schools become part of the community.

This is especially the situation with this facility, where it will function more as a community center and not just a school that closes at the end of the day," the newsletter noted that. Both the committee and the school's incoming principal William 'Wes' McAllister agreed students would wear uniforms, black pants or skirts, along with white shirts or blouses, to create a sense of pride and harmony among students.

The school's vision is to adhere to the adage *'It takes a village to raise a child.'* And has expanded this adage to *'It takes a village to help any of its inhabitants grow.'*

The new $25 million dollar middle school in its first year enrolled 700 pupils. After 5 years, an educational assessment of the school identified needed changes in crucial areas impairing the school's ability to improve.

Educators, Marie Cianca and Paul Lampe reported in

198

Principal Leadership that in 2000, Dr. Freddie Thomas Learning Center had been labeled a '*school under registration review*' by the New York State Education Department and was under a directive to make significant progress or face serious consequences.

Three years later in 2003, only 3 percent of 8th students were meeting state standards in mathematics and only 9 percent in English language arts. The school climate was no better. Within the first five years, three different principals were appointed to Thomas. The frequent changes in leadership did not allow for a consistent instructional vision or clear procedures for keeping order in the building. After only two years, 3/4 of the staff had to be replaced because of transfers out of school and increasing enrollment.

Many of the new hires were inexperienced first-year teachers. The severity of the Education Department's citation prompted the school district to reconfigure and "grow out" the middle school to grades 7-12.

With a sense of urgency, the Rochester Board of Education unanimously approved a nearly $1 million dollars plan. The plan will cover changes to administrative positions within the school. The remaining funds will pay for additional staffing and resources, such as math and bilingual teachers and a new sentry.

"What I want to look at is getting off the 'school under registration review' list, but also how we can make learning better for all city middle schools," Principal Donna Gattelaro-Andersen said. "Students now change rooms just three times a day instead of as many as ten times. The number of lunch periods has been reduced from four to two. And instructional periods are 85 minutes instead of 37," she added. "Reducing the amount of time students spend outside classrooms, cut the number of incidents requiring disciplinary action and teachers were moved into areas in which they are certified instead of teaching subjects that were not their specialties."

The Freddie Thomas Foundation Board of Directors approved a proposal submitted by Midge to support the school's overhaul in the following areas:

• Beautifying the school exterior through Rochester City School District's office staff;

• Recruit qualified mentors for the children

• Provide awards for student achievements

• Solicit gifts and opportunities to honor roll students

• Maintain professionally the motif of the two Freddie Thomas showcases

• Stimulate the school's public relations image to individuals and organizations

• Support parent participation projects and programs

• Recruit motivational speakers at the request of school staff

• Identify a school staff member to serve on the Freddie Thomas Foundation Board of Directors.

In February 2002, Midge partnered with the school's University of Rochester extension to create, The Freddie Thomas University of Rochester Science Award.

"The annual award is awarded to a student who meets and exceeds the school's expectations for students," Midge said. "This student shall resemble a likeness to Dr. Freddie Thomas in that he or she is a scholar who has served the school in a positive way. And a person who participates in community service projects, participates in school activities, is friendly, shows a caring attitude, is concern for the welfare of others and encourages others to do the same. In addition, the recipient is a well-rounded person who has established himself or herself as a peacemaker and has achieved academically."

In July, Midge launched the beautification project encompassing the school's front entrance. Students from Edison Tech and Thomas planted the trees and shrubs.

Several months into the project, Officer Allen Smith died in a motorcycle accident on his way to Thomas, where he was stationed. His death inspired board members of the Freddie Thomas Foundation to sponsor a memorial garden in his honor, as part of the beautification project.

"Al Smith was a role model to many neighborhood children as well as adults," Midge said. "He had a sense of humor and he shared his great athletic skills in volunteering as a coach for the softball team. His passion was to uplift the conditions of males, he was associated with."

Later that year in December, Midge met with Dr. William Cala over concerns of the school's heavy dropout rate; issues of low parent involvement and to put into place a plan of action.

With the assistance of Dr. Bruce Gilberg, an executive director of a mentoring program for city and suburban students, Freddie Thomas High School Ambassadors Program was initiated.

Forty-three ambassadors from the Rochester community were invited to work with parents and as custodial guardians of the students. The goal and mission of the program was to actively engage adult members of the families and be participants in the educational process of their children. Ambassadors were to listen to parent concerns and assist with problem solving and resolutions.

The gender breakdown was 23 adult male volunteers and 23 adult female volunteers. All ambassadors were African Americans. Each ambassador was asked to commit to working with three families and to make personal contact with each family for a minimum of once a week.

In an article, *Mentoring can inspire families*: Democrat and Chronicle Conversation Editor Cynthia Benjamin said, outside a room at Dr. Freddie Thomas High School, she heard youthful laughter and chatter from the hallway as students switch classes.

"Inside the room, I sat among a group of mentors from the community," Benjamin said. "We were at the school to discuss several goals, namely how we can inspire students to stay in school and earn their diplomas. The school's principal Sandra Jordan knows the goals are within reach, because every senior at Freddie Thomas received diplomas for the 2006-07 school years."

"Midge Thomas hopes the ambassadors will connect with

families and use their life experiences to inspire parents," Benjamin said. "Midge is pleased, so many people have stepped up, but more people are needed; particularly to assist Latino families."

"This is what Freddie was doing," Midge added. "When he met youngsters, he ended up meeting their moms and dads, so the families felt comfortable. He was mentoring families."

After three years the ambassador program was assessed for its effectiveness by the city school district. The final assessment report stated that:

• The teachers these students were assigned to noted a marked improvement with their overall attendance;

• The students showed an increased interest in their assignments and were submitting more homework;

• Parental contacts to the school were of more of a concern and engagement and not a defensive interaction.

"Six years later in 2009, the principal of Dr. Freddie Thomas High School and a representative team of teachers and administrators were on stage at the Teachers College of Columbia University receiving the *Panasonic National School Change Award,* the Principal Leadership reported. "To receive this award, the school provided evidence of significant change in attitudes, beliefs, and values; instructional practices; achievement; stakeholder perceptions and student engagement."

Each year, between 60 and 100 schools is nominated for the National School Change Award. Twenty-four finalists are named, and only 6 of those are chosen by a national panel to receive the award.

Dr. Freddie Thomas High School is the first secondary school in the Rochester City School District to win this award and the only high school in the entire country selected for the award that year. The school dramatically improved overall performance over the last 5 years, particularly in the areas of graduation rates, math and English language arts scores, and long-term and short-term suspensions.

Since the creation of a new leadership team, Thomas:

• Has experienced two school years, 2007 and 2008, its first two years of having a senior graduating class, where the graduation rate was 100 percent;

• Has increased the percentage of students meeting New York State targets for math from 3 percent in 2003-2004 to 64 percent in 2007-2008;

• Has increased the percentage of students meeting New York State targets for English Language Arts from 12 percent in 2003-2004 to 43 percent in 2007-2008;

• Has decreased the number of long-term suspensions from 150 in 2003-2004 to 40 in 2007-2008;

• Has decreased the number of short-term suspensions from 932 in 2002-2003 to 200 in 2007-2008.

"The ambassador program was developed around Freddie's philosophy," Midge said. "The academic turnaround at Thomas in 2008, underscores how Freddie's philosophy could be used today to improve underperforming schools housed in poverty-stricken city districts."

Former and current principals at Thomas have continued to celebrate and promote Freddie's legacy and philosophy at the school. The school sponsors Dr. Freddie Thomas Week, an annual event that's scheduled during the week of his birthday.

The five-day event includes:

• Monday- opening day, guest speakers and former students of Freddie Thomas share their experiences under his tutelage

• Tuesday-Scientist and Inventor Day; local scientists and engineers share knowledge about the S.T.E.M. fields

• Wednesday- Community Day; volunteers from the community share experiences and engage the students

• Thursday- Career Day; volunteers of various professions share information and experiences about their careers

• Friday-College Bound Day; college officials share information about preparing for college.

Dr. Freddie Thomas Learning Center, 625 Scio Street,

Rochester, New York

A SMILE

(A poem)

Hold back not a smile that you have for me today, give
them a pleasant smile to keep cheerful, as you meet daily
on life's highway.

If my little song has helped someone today, I hope
someone's heart has been made to feel glad, may sorrows
pass and happiness come true with my little song I have
tried to sing.

By Dr. Freddie L. Thomas 1918-1974

Epilogue

Freddie was committed to making the lives of others and the communities he shared better. In the 56 years he lived, he excelled in more fields in one lifetime than most people would in 2 or 3.

He was a historian and a scientist, an inventor and an author, a book collector, a composer, and a scholar. He was known as an authority in Afro-American and Jewish cultural history. Many still remember his home on Skuse Street as a center of learning, discussion and inspiration for the community.

In trying to compensate for his many contributions to humanity, I've chosen a letter from his archives, dated March 6, 1973, addressed to Freddie from The Reverend Walter G. Smihula, Pastor of Saint John English Evangelical Church in Lynbrook, New York.

Smihula writes:

"I know this letter will seem to be like 'a voice from the distant past. After all, we have not seen one another for approximately twenty tears. I deeply regret that loss of contact. However, I do cherish many memories of our time at Wagner, and the few months that we shared at the

Rochester Y.M.C.A. In all of this, I fondly remember that
we enjoyed the precious gift of friendship. I am, of course,
writing as a result of the article in the recent issue of The
Alumni Magazine. I must confess that I reacted to the
material with mixed emotions. It was wonderful to read
about your personal achievements, and the community
projects in which you have been engaged. Frankly, neither
came as a surprise; particularly your fruitful involvement
with other people. The capacity to brighten the lives of
those around you has always been in evidence. The news of
your illness temporarily left me a little breathless. Yet, the
feeling could not remain. You see, I also have the
conviction 'quality' and not 'quantity' is the real hallmark
of human existence. Life is not simply measured in days or
years, but in-terms of how life's moments have been used.
During my ministry, I have had the opportunity to witness
the truth of that reality. I have known too many people who
have attained longevity, without ever really understanding
the beauty of living. I have also seen those who crowded a
much shorter life span with an abundance of meaningful
and satisfying experiences. No person has a choice
regarding the time of his departure and certainly, no more
than the time of his arrival. Nevertheless, we can all choose
the kind of lifestyle that stands between the events of birth

and death. Permit me to say as a friend: You have chosen well."

My Dear Freddie:

It has been a long time (over forty years) and I've continued to be overwhelmed and inspired with the legacy you've created. I am cherishing another opportunity to write a letter to you because it's powerful and meaningful therapy. Afterwards, I am just fine.

In this letter, I am reflecting on some of those seventeen precious years and two weeks of our lives together. I recall you teasing dad and mother to give you another Midge. Well, I've been looking for a clone of Freddie L. Thomas but I haven't found him yet. However, cherishing fond memories of you are enough for me.

Honey, today is September 9, 2014, and on the 9th day of each month, I still think about those, *'I Love You'* cards with jewelry, perfume, lingerie, and the small station wagon, formal gowns, the mink coat and so on.

I remember when we would shop at the public market on Saturdays, divide the fruits and veggies and then deliver them to friends who had children. Oh yes! I will never forget how we laughed and talked to each other so much on our monthly trips that once, you missed an exit in Pennsylvania and we ended up in Princeton, New Jersey and decided to visit my cousins. Well, I could go on and on.

Besides the many precious memories, I specifically remember the day you said your dream was to own the downtown old

Jewish community center building at 380 Andrews Street.

Clearly, you were still in our thoughts and actions when we made it happen after you left us by establishing, The Freddie Thomas Foundation, Inc. Our archives are testimonies of the celebration when we installed the foundation's cornerstone and renaming the former Jewish Community Center, Triangle Community Center on September 27, 1974.

By the way, I think it was you who inspired or suggested to the book's project manager, Rodney Brown and LaShay Harris to title your biography, '*Silent Leader*'

We know that you didn't want pomp and circumstance over what truly came from your heart. We appreciate and thank you for all you've done by reaching-out and sharing your generous unselfish wisdom.

Freddie, you were a blessing to many of us. I believe and anticipate by reading *Silent Leader*; many will continue to be inspired to greatness by being a blessing to others.

Love,

Midge

Dr. Thomas and Midge attending her brother, Charles's wedding (June 1968)

Give Me Your Hand

-Written and composed by Freddie L. Thomas-

-Lyrics of their wedding song, dedicated to Midge
'February 9,'1957'-

Give me your hand, as now I stand beside you

Give me your hand, my life, my love divine give me your
hand, and let my love provide you with all you need, to
build God a shrine

Not Just for now, but forever and a day not just so far, but
all along the way Nothing have I, but this true love to give
only to you as long as we shall live give me your hand as
now I stand beside you

Give me your hand and I'll give you my heart

Take thou my hand, as now I stand beside you take thou
my hand, my life, my love devine take thou my hand, and
let my love provide you with all you need to build to God a
shrine

Not just for now, but ever and a day not just so far, but all
along the way

Nothing has I, but this true love to give only to you as long as we shall live

Take thou my hand, as now I stand beside you take thou my hand, and I'll give you my heart.

Proceeds from the biography will supplement funds needed to re invigorate the legacy of Dr. Thomas.

Please continue to visit us at *www.drfreddiethomas.com* or *Facebook.com@Silent Leader* to keep track of scheduled events, including book signings and discussions about the legacy of Dr. Freddie Thomas.

Selected Bibliography

➤ Adams, Archie: *Freddie L. Thomas: A, Personal Memoir*, 1974, Rochester, NY.

➤ Benjamin, Cynthia: *Mentoring Can Inspire Families,* Democrat and Chronicle, Rochester, NY, Sunday, November 18, 2007.

➤ Black Business Network: *Marcus Garvey*, Tag Team Marketing International 2014.

➤ Black History Museum Umum Newsletter, *Scientifically Black: Freddie L. Thomas, Brilliant Black Cytologist and Historian, Philadelphia, Pennsylvania, April 1973.*

➤ Blair, Henry: *A Brief History of the University of Rochester Atomic Energy Project 1943-1968,* Rochester, NY.

➤ Buyer, Dan: *City School Board honors 'teacher's teacher Thomas*, Rochester Free Press, Rochester, NY, Friday, May 12, 1995.

➤ Cato, David John, Ph.D., *Letter to Freddie*, March 6, 1973.

➢ Cianca, Marie and Lampe, Paul: *Restoring Hope,* Principal Leadership, Rochester, NY September 2010.

➢ City of Rochester: *Brief Bio of Freddie L. Thomas,* Sesquicentennial Committee, Rochester, NY, June 9,1984.

➢ Daniels, Ray: *My Thoughts of Freddie Thomas,* Rochester, NY 2012.

➢ Department of Radiation Biology and Biophysics: *The University of Rochester Atomic Energy Project,* Rochester, NY 1968.

➢ Democrat and Chronicle: *Interview with Mrs. Harper Sibley* [Grande Dames Who Grace America], Rochester, NY June 1, 1967, June 12, 1980.

➢ Dupree, Adolph: *Black History Exhibit Marks Beginning of Permanent Library for The Freddie L. Thomas Collection,* (Press Release) Rochester, NY, March 5, 1980.

➢ Engle D. Dresden*" Pittman Stand for Equality, Freedom,* The Brighton-Pittsford Post, Rochester, NY, Thursday, June 1, 1989.

➢ Griffin, John: *Biography of Freddie L. Thomas,*

Eulogistic Service Interfaith Chapel University of Rochester, Rochester, NY, March 3, 1974.

➤ Marketview Heights News: *Freddie Thomas Learning Center's Middle School named at Ceremony,* community newsletter of South Marketview Heights, Rochester, NY, June 1995.

➤ Monroe Community College, All College Committee: *Consultation on Black Studies and interested students,* (Minutes from meeting) Rochester, NY, October 13, 1970.

➤ Morris, Brian: *The Legend of Freddie Thomas is Alive in Rochester,* Wagner College Magazine, Staten Island, NY, winter 1973.

➤ Norfolk Journal and Guide: *Life of Henri Christophe Told at UNIA Meeting,* Norfolk, Virginia, September 28, 1945.

➤ Norfolk Journal and Guide: *Race History Library Dedicated*-[Speakers Cite Group Record] Norfolk, Virginia, June 23, 1945.

➤ PBS American Experience: Marcus Garvey, 1999-2000.

➤ River Campus Libraries: *Franklin Florence Papers,* University of Rochester, Rare Books, Special

Collection and Preservation, Rochester, NY 1962-1972.

➢ Rochester City School District: *Dr. Freddie Thomas High School Wins Prestigious National School Change Award*, Rochester, NY, April 29, 2009.

➢ Shabazz Ray: *Jewels of the Genesee*, Genesee Valley Sefekh/Sesheta M.H.Z. Publication, Rochester, NY, Second Printing, March 2002.

➢ Smihula G. Walter, Rev: *Letter to Freddie*, March 6, 1973.

➢ Staten Island Advance: *Negro Race History Told at Meeting* [Originated in Pacific Area Student Tells NAACP Youth Group], Staten Island, NY, August 10, 1949.

➢ The American National Standards: Film Structure, Kodak.com, Rochester, NY 2004.

➢ The Harvard Crimson: *Med School Dean Lauds Performance of Roxbury Educational Organization*, Roxbury, Massachusetts, March 3, 1973.

➢ The NAACP Norfolk and Portsmouth, Virginia 1920-1940: *Race Consciousness and the Legal Offensive*, Norfolk, Virginia, December 1, 2000.

➤ Thomas L. Freddie: *History of the African in Asia,* The Empire State, Buffalo, NY, [series: June 6, 1957, to December 19, 1958.

➤ Thompson, Shirley: *A Proud History, A Bright Future,* Frederick Douglass Voice, Rochester, NY, November 9, 1994

➤ Thomas, Shirley: *Freddie Thomas Foundation Celebrates 20th Year,* Frederick Douglass Voice, Rochester, NY, November 9, 1994.

➤ University of Rochester: *Report of the Residential College Commission Subcommittee on Diversity,* Rochester, NY, March 1999.

➤ Wagner College, Alumni Link: *Letter from Freddie,* Wagner College Magazine, Staten Island, NY, spring 1972.

➤ West's Encyclopedia of American Law, edition 2: *Black Power Movement, 2008.*

➤ Willingham, Breea: *Freddie Thomas Plan Goes Forward,* Democrat and Chronicle, Rochester, NY, October 23, 2000.

Rodney Brown and Midge Thomas-Rochester Black

Heritage Pioneer Award Ceremony (2012)

Made in the USA
Middletown, DE
02 December 2020